And Then She Was Happy

And Then She Was Happy

A BOOK ABOUT DIVORCE

Kristi Skordahl

BEAVER'S
POND
PRESS

ISBN 13: 978-1-59298-567-8

Library of Congress Catalog Number: 2012919055

Printed in the United States of America

First Printing: 2013

17 16 15 14 13   5 4 3 2 1

Cover design by Emily Mahon
Interior design and typesetting by James Monroe Design, LLC.
Design assistance by Kristina Fong
Author photo by Valérie Jardin

BEAVER'S
POND
PRESS

Beaver's Pond Press
7108 Ohms Lane
Edina, MN 55439–2129
952-829-8818
www.BeaversPondPress.com

To order, visit www.BeaversPondBooks.com
or call 1-800-901-3480. Reseller discounts available.

*To the "lanterns," who have shined light on my path
and helped me find my way.
I truly believe we are in this world
to help one another heal.
Thank you for helping me.
And to my clients, who show me every day
what it is to be strong, courageous, and true
to our best selves in exceptionally
challenging circumstances.*

DISCARD

Contents

PART ONE: What I Lived

The Greenhouse 1

South Dakota 9

The Ballroom of Stone 21

The Hospital 31

And Then She Was Happy 41

Lawyering Up 45

Moving Forward 49

Enough 59

And Then She Went Back to Work 63

Miraval 69

Our Common Pain 81

PART TWO: What I Learned

Trust Your Gut 87

Give Your Partner an Opportunity to Change 91

Accept Responsibility 95

Gather Support 99

Assemble Your Professional Team 101

Tame Your Greek Chorus 109

Manage Worry 113

Take Charge of Your Finances 117

Accept Realignment 123

Claim Your Territory (and Choose Your Battles) . . . 127

Make Good Choices 133

Recognize Your Blind Spots 139

Look at the Big Picture 143

Pursue Happiness 149

This story is true.
Some names and minor facts
were altered to protect
identities and facilitate storytelling.

How long the road is.
But for all the time the journey has already taken,
how you have needed every second of it
in order to learn what the road passes by.

—DAG HAMMARSKJÖLD

Part One

WHAT I LIVED

Many years ago, I read an article written by an accomplished brain surgeon who, after many years of practice, found *himself* in need of brain surgery. Despite this man's exhaustive training and experience, when he got the news about his own condition, he was paralyzed. He had absolutely no idea how to transition from healer to patient, and it took him a great deal of time, distress, and personal transformation to move forward. Ultimately, he successfully made the transition, and when all was said and done, the experience changed everything about how he lived his life and how he practiced medicine.

I had a similar experience when, after many years as a divorce attorney, I found myself facing a divorce of my own. When this reality hit me, my first reaction was, "What do I do now?"

Of course, I knew what to *do*. I had managed dozens and dozens of divorces, and I had mastered the legal technicalities of divorce. I could handle a case with surgical precision. I knew where to place the incisions. I knew how to stitch them up. And I knew how to manage the post-op details. I knew "everything" about going through a divorce. Still, there I was—so consumed with my own pain and loss that every bit of legal knowledge I possessed felt entirely irrelevant.

Eventually, I did make the transition from attorney to client. Along the way, I made some good choices and some not-so-good choices, but I got to the other side in one solid piece. And like the brain surgeon's experience, my experience changed everything about how I live my life and how I practice law.

This is the story of what I lived before, during, and after the most difficult transition of my life.

The Greenhouse

I married much later in life than I had expected, but when it happened, I knew the timing was exactly right.

We met on a blind date. The match was brokered by colleagues at our respective law firms, and the inspiration was that I loved horses and Mel's alter ego was a cowboy. Mel's law office was decorated full-out cowboy. He had saddles in the entryway and western art on all the walls, and his conference table was adorned with imprints from a branding iron. Although he drove a sports car and lived in the middle of Saint Paul, he referred to himself as "the cowboy lawyer."

The date broker on my end was Scott, an attorney at my firm whose office was next to mine. Although younger than me, Scott was like the big brother I never had. He was more interested in getting me married than I was. While Scott had a picture of his wife and kids on his desk, I had a picture of a horse I once met. Scott was determined to change that. The broker on Mel's end was an associate at his own law firm who probably expected he would earn big points with the boss if he found him an appropriate match.

I was still licking wounds from a long-ago heartbreak, and I had not dated for several years. But with the enthusiastic support of my matchmaker, I agreed to give it a shot.

Mel and I met for lunch at one of those restaurants that has paper tablecloths and crayons on each table. When I first saw him, my heart sank. He just looked too old, too flashy, and too not my type. He was wearing a bright yellow double-breasted jacket and cowboy boots. His hair was slicked back against his head, and it looked suspiciously as if it had been dyed. He looked more like an eccentric uncle than a date.

It turned out that Mel was only eight years older than me (he was fifty at the time), but he looked much older. He had been married for nineteen years, then single for nine, and he had three grown children. Mel had a lot more life under his belt than I did, and it showed.

As we sat down to lunch, however, we soon found ourselves deep in a conversation about, of all things, cattle herding strategies. We drew diagrams on the paper tablecloth and spoke passionately about our differing opinions on the matter.

My infrequent and hard-earned time off from my law practice almost always involved horses in some manner, and I had recently returned from a cattle drive in Nevada. Mel had done similar work in his home state of South Dakota. Needless to say, it was unusual to find an intelligent, single man working in downtown Minneapolis who had any interest whatsoever in cattle herding. When I spoke of the thrill of waking up in the morning to see a herd of horses galloping over the crest of a hill, Mel got it. He spoke my language. Soon Mel's "oldness" and "flashiness" faded to the background. He was interesting.

We lunched long into the afternoon, and as he walked me back to my office, we decided our next date would take place on the backs of horses. It did, and in the weeks and months that followed, we became nearly inseparable.

It was not just our horse connection that attracted me to Mel. He had a way about him that conveyed protection. I had never felt truly protected by anyone in my life, so I was drawn to him.

Mel wooed me aggressively. He took me to cowboy bars and taught me how to two-step. We took motorcycling lessons. We rode horses in Arizona, and we played blackjack in Las Vegas. It was nonstop fun, and I was having the time of my life.

I was happier than I had been in years. I was loving my work, I was loving my life, and I was falling in love with Mel.

About six months into our relationship, however, I started to feel some unfamiliar and persistent knee pain.

Soon the pain spread to my hands and feet. Within a few months, all my joints were aching, and every move I made was painful. The pain seemed to come out of nowhere, and I struggled with it for many weeks before I found a specialist who could see me.

When I finally got an appointment, my diagnosis was clear: rheumatoid arthritis. My rheumatologist started me on an assortment of drug regimens in an effort to get the pain under control, but nothing helped. Meanwhile, I felt as if my life was being sucked right out of me. Joy and ambition took a backseat to pain management. The disease soon began to affect my work.

I practiced family law at a highly regarded Minneapolis firm, and I loved my work. It wasn't just a job to me; it was a calling. Early in my practice, I had worked in numerous areas of the law. I found most of them interesting, but over time, I found myself undeniably drawn to family law. While many attorneys find family law distasteful, I found it irresistible. I was intensely curious about family dynamics, and it was gratifying to be invited into people's lives and have the opportunity to help them during a time of deep personal struggle.

I was happy and successful. But now I was struggling with a painful, chronic disease that changed all my expectations about my future.

Many days, I could not sign my own name. I was often unable to wear shoes. My secretary, Cathy, and my paralegal, Lisa, signed my letters and bought me comfy slippers to wear around the office. Many times, I would just close my office door and cry. I was so frustrated.

One morning when I had an early court appearance, I got out of bed and found myself physically unable to lift the toilet seat. I called Lisa on speed dial in a panic. I had no idea how I could possibly get dressed, much less get to court and do my job. Lisa talked me through the next few minutes, and with her support, I fought through the pain, got myself together, and managed to get to the courthouse on time.

After that, on nights before early court appearances, I would wake myself up in the middle of the night in order to have sufficient time to loosen up my joints. Obviously, this only made my already-bad health worse.

When my doctor recommended I take some time off, I resisted at first. But I knew that continuing to work while battling this disease would eventually take a much larger toll on my physical and emotional health. The day I told my firm I was taking disability leave was one of the worst days of my life. I felt as if I were letting everyone down. But the firm offered me unwavering support.

And so did Mel. Mel was undeterred by my declining physical condition. I managed to keep him shielded from the worst of it, but as my health deteriorated, Mel's commitment deepened. He seemed attracted to my helplessness.

By this time, I was deeply in love with Mel, and I did not want to burden him with my illness. But Mel wanted to get married, and he was persistent about it. He proposed marriage on New Year's Eve 1999 in Las Vegas. We were married a few months later.

Mel loved being my rescuer and it was a role he excelled in. He gave me space to manage my illness without guilt or financial worry. Mel earned a good income, and my disability insurer settled my claim with a fairly large lump-sum payment, so we were in fine shape financially without my income. Also, as Mel's wife, I was covered by his medical insurance—which was a big concern for me at the time. I was completely broken physically, and Mel offered his support with a generosity I had never before experienced. Our relationship was wonderful on so many levels.

But as time went on, I started to sense an emptiness I could not pinpoint. In her short story "What Is Seized," writer Lorrie Moore describes something I felt at the time but could not yet articulate. I started to sense that Mel's caregiving was "something brought out for show—something annexed to his soul like a fake greenhouse where I thought I saw life and vitality and sun and greenness." Cracks in our "greenhouse" started appearing very early in our marriage, and over time, they became increasingly difficult to ignore.

Although my illness continued to be a challenge, I had enough functional hours in the day to take care of the house and the laundry and the grocery shopping and the cooking. Mel finally had the housewife he needed, and although I remained frustrated with my limitations, I was relieved that I no longer had to manage the additional stress of my job.

Two years into our marriage, my rheumatologist struck gold with an intravenous medication. I started to feel relief almost immediately after my first infusion. After several months of treatment, my health was largely restored, and I felt ready to return to work. I would likely remain on this drug for the rest of my life, but three hours in a recliner every few weeks with an IV in my arm and a stack of trashy magazines in my lap was an easy investment to be free from the debilitating pain that had defined the last three years of my life.

But as my body started to heal, Mel began voicing resistance to the idea of me returning to work. By now, I was deeply entrenched in our life together, and Mel depended upon me for just about everything other than earning income. Mel wanted me to continue taking care of our Saint Paul home and the ranch we were planning in South Dakota. He also wanted me to remain available to accompany him on frequent trips related to his own law practice and to tend to our numerous social and charitable obligations.

Mel needed a lot of attention, and I soon realized there would never be enough room in our marriage for two busy trial lawyers. Although I missed my work a great deal, I was still enormously grateful to Mel, and I was committed to making our marriage work. I was so in love with our greenhouse that I was willing to let the other great love of my life—family law—fall to the wayside.

Lorrie Moore continues with the metaphor that was becoming my life:

> *And then when you love them, they lead you*
> *out [of the greenhouse] and into their real soul.*
> *A drafty, cavernous, empty ballroom, inexorably*
> *arched and vaulted and mocking you with its*
> *echoes—you hear all you have sacrificed, all you*
> *have given, landing on the floor with a loud clunk.*
> *They lock the greenhouse and you are as tiny*
> *as a figure in an architect's drawing, a faceless*
> *splotch, a blur of stick limbs abandoned in some*
> *voluminous desert of stone.*

South Dakota

I kind of resented my first twenty-seven trips to South Dakota. Blinded by love, I had married a man who would not miss a kindergarten reunion, family birthday party, or church bake sale in his hometown in the northeastern corner of the state. We once drove five hours from our Saint Paul home to judge a hands-free-beer-bottle-opening contest.

The first few trips were manageable. I love the South Dakota prairie. Although I grew up in the suburbs of Minneapolis, both of my parents grew up on Depression-era family farms in the Midwest—my mom's was in Pigeon Falls, Wisconsin, and my dad's was in Sinai, South Dakota. I feel a deep connection with both farms, but there is something about the South Dakota prairie that really gets to me. Where others might see miles and miles of nothing, I see wide-open space where my heart and mind can breathe. Every time I find myself on the prairie, my entire being exhales. In those early years with Mel, however, being on the prairie was anything but liberating.

While I drove on those long trips back and forth between Saint Paul and South Dakota, Mel sat in the passenger seat, tending to his work. There was little conversation, no radio, no books on tape. Just hour after hour of Mel barking into his phone, complaining about the cell service, and offering a hand gesture here and there to indicate his needs: food, drink, restroom.

Upon arrival, we settled into the basement of his parents' small house and would then be immediately thrown into the family agenda for the weekend. Church events, school events, lots of parties, lots of beer, lots of family stories, and endless games of bridge—a game I played poorly, which annoyed Mel tremendously.

Mel's family members had a very high opinion of themselves. Although the Bradys lived modest lives by most standards, there was a palpable sense that they thought they were better than other people. I knew my acceptance in this family—which I very much wanted—was fully conditional on complete loyalty to their way of life. So as had been my habit, I did what was expected of me cheerfully and without complaint.

The family often lightheartedly referred to their long list of family rules as "The Brady Policy Manual." I soon learned that this policy manual was no joke. This was serious business, and I learned the rules by being continually corrected on my mistakes.

Once while cheering for my nephew at his high

school basketball game, I stood up after he made an amazing field goal and yelled, "Go, Stevie!" Sitting beside me, Mel's sister looked embarrassed and alarmed. She touched my arm, brought me back to my seat, looked me in the eyes, and very patiently and earnestly explained that I should not cheer for Stevie. Rather, I should cheer for the color of his team—blue. This was proper Brady cheering, and I was expected to cheer appropriately.

Another time, I invited a neighbor to dinner over the phone, telling her she was "more than welcome" to join us. After I hung up, Mel instructed me to call her back and tell her she was "warmly welcomed" to dinner, because the Bradys didn't use the expression "more than welcome." It just wasn't the right way to invite someone to dinner.

I accepted the coaching compliantly, took note of each Brady policy, and made certain that Stevie never received another direct cheer and that nobody was ever "more than welcome" again. I noted rule after rule after rule, and after a couple of years, I was functioning as a fairly convincing Brady. It was a lot of work, and the most intensive training took place during those twenty-seven trips to South Dakota.

But on that fateful twenty-eighth trip, my captivity in the Brady lifestyle started to loosen. On a beautiful Saturday afternoon, Mel and I drove forty miles northwest of his hometown to visit one of his childhood friends, Corrine, who along with her husband had recently taken over management of a ranch on five hundred acres of high prairie lands above the Red River Valley. As we turned into the long driveway to Prairie Sky Guest and Game Ranch, we entered a landscape that grabbed my heart.

The sky was so impossibly big. The land seemed to extend forever. Dozens of horses and hundreds of bison dotted the horizon. It was breathtaking. In just a few moments, everything about South Dakota returned to the peaceful place it had been for me before Mel. I felt at home. It was my first and only experience with love at first sight.

Within a few months of that first visit, Mel and I purchased some neglected land just one mile down the road from Prairie Sky and neatly notched into its bison pastures. We cleared this desolate tract of its abandoned sheds and untended trees and found ourselves with a bare but promising sixteen acres of mud. From these humble beginnings, we planned our beautiful "lake home without the lake," which was how we explained our endeavor to our Minnesota friends in a way they could understand.

No longer practicing law, and with my arthritis now largely under control, I was desperate for a new project. So I poured all my energy into our South Dakota ranch. Over the next year, we created what I still consider to be the most sacred place on earth. While Mel tended to his law practice, I managed the day-to-day responsibility of building our ranch. We christened it Two Star.

Although Two Star was small, we wanted everything about it to be perfect. The Internet offered thousands upon thousands of choices for every last detail, and I believe I looked at and considered every last one of them. I spent hours every day searching for the perfect light fixtures, the perfect rugs, and the perfect bed linens.

With the help of our contractor, I laid out the floor plans for the log house and the barn. I selected interior doors from Maine, porch furniture from South Carolina, and custom dining room furnishings from Tennessee. And true to my Norwegian roots, I purchased all of it at the best possible prices. I worked with a woman in New Mexico to design handmade quilts for the beds. I selected every appliance, door hinge, doorknob, window, and door. Every book, every glass, every knife, fork, and spoon in that place I chose with great care.

As the barn was framed and the log home began rising from the mud, I kept watch over every detail. Although my arthritis reared up now and then, it did not slow me down. I painted the hitching posts and hand-finished the walls in the barn. I planted the pine shrubs and raspberry bushes bordering the house and barn. I bought a handmade wooden swing for the front pasture and cleared a walking path and fire pit. My heart and soul permeated that place. We were ecstatic about Two Star.

With Two Star in the works, Mel and I had the

opportunity to own horses—a dream we had each long held. First came Ned, a feisty-but-sweet red sorrel that Mel quickly claimed as his own. Soon Ted joined the family. Ted was a big, beautiful dark brown bay with a gorgeous black mane and the most amazing rump I have ever seen on any being on this earth. Ted was assigned to me. He was my big, beautiful boy. Eventually Roy, Bob, and Star rounded out our herd.

Ted and I had a somewhat tempestuous start to our relationship. He always regarded me coolly and with an air of annoyance. While the other horses huddled around me for cookies and affection, Ted rebuffed my advances. He was not easily seduced. As soon as he saw me enter the pasture, he immediately and very deliberately walked to a far corner and turned his impressive rump in my direction. It was his cute, horsey way of giving me the finger.

Early on, Ted tossed me off his back fairly frequently and seemed to take enormous satisfaction in doing so. I also suffered the fairly regular *accidental* step on the foot or the *unintentional* 1,300-pound body check. When I wanted to ride, I had to try every trick in the book to catch Ted in the pasture. Sometimes he and I spent hours engaged in what seemed like a determined power struggle—woman versus beast.

Often, just when I thought I had Ted cornered with no way out, he would make a sudden turn and trot right past me. Thinking back on these standoffs, I still feel the familiar stir in my heart that I used to feel whenever he'd brush by me. It was a combination of abject frustration and unabashed admiration for his intelligence and beauty. He was testing me, and I wanted to prove myself worthy.

Of course, I could have given up and ridden another horse, but I didn't want to just *ride*. I wanted to *ride Ted*. Sometimes I caught him; sometimes I didn't. But I didn't give up. I came back to that pasture day after day, and I think my determination finally won him over. Despite a few bumps and bruises to my body and my ego, Ted and I eventually reached an understanding, and we developed a deep bond.

Ted soon became the equine love of my life—and although I like to believe that he might have loved me back, our relationship would probably be more accurately described as "unconditional positive regard." He was never outwardly warm to me, but over time I found a connection in his eyes. I felt an alert responsiveness from him when we rode, and once our initial troubles were behind us, he exhibited an unrelenting and selfless determination to protect me.

Rather than allow me to take what was sure to be an ugly and painful fall while trying to jump a swollen creek, Ted would make a sudden and probably painful shift to his body and manage to keep me upright. He never expected credit for these saves, but he knew that I knew he had saved me. At the end of the day, Ted tried his best to resist enjoying the extra brushing and grain I offered him, but inevitably, our eyes would meet with the acknowledgement that we were a team.

But as Two Star blossomed, the cracks in the "greenhouse" of our marriage widened. I had been introduced to Mel's temper fairly early in our relationship, but back then, his episodes were infrequent enough to not cause me great alarm. After we married, however, they increased in frequency and intensity.

The seemingly smallest things would trigger Mel: a telephone that was not hung up correctly (I was undermining his business), a bag of dog food I didn't remember leaving in his car (I was calling him a liar), a prescription bottle placed on the wrong shelf in his medicine cabinet (I was trying to kill him).

His rage was completely unpredictable. I tried endlessly to talk things through with him, but my efforts accomplished nothing other than to leave me exhausted with frustration and helplessness. Soon I was walking through my life on eggshells, wanting nothing more than to keep Mel happy and his rage at bay.

When Mel was happy, he was the nicest fellow on earth. He was gregarious and generous and full of fun and affection. But when I said the wrong thing or did something that didn't win his approval, Mel didn't take a breath before attacking me—and I was simply not emotionally equipped to handle his attacks.

Although friends and family members witnessed

Mel's episodes from time to time, no useful help was offered from any direction. No one ever called him on his behavior. Everyone in our world seemed to bow down to Mel, and I was left to wonder if there was something terribly wrong with my perception of reality.

I found myself relying on Ted for the unconditional acceptance and protection I craved from Mel. Ted didn't care about the extra pounds gathering around my middle-aged waist or the fact that I wasn't always freshly showered or wearing makeup. He neither wanted nor expected accolades and praise when he helped me through a rough patch. He never reminded me of the constant mistakes I made while trying to navigate the prairie with him, and we ended each day with unspoken appreciation, unrelenting forgiveness, and deep respect.

Life in South Dakota kept me sane. During and after Two Star's construction, I engaged myself deeply in the lives of our neighbors. I helped birth the calves and lambs that were their lifeblood. I spent glorious—and often arduous—days and nights branding their cattle, sorting their calves, shearing their sheep, and even frying up a few Rocky Mountain oysters to enjoy with ice-cold PBR after a busy day of castrating bulls (a useful skill, I might add). I judged the annual rodeo queen contest. I was the substitute organist at the church in our tiny town of Veblen. I found a home in my heart and a place I cherished in this world. I was no longer just Mel's wife; I was a part of the community.

Mel had an office in Minneapolis and a home office at Two Star, so we traveled back and forth frequently—always wanting to spend as much time at Two Star as possible. Mel and I hosted frequent dinners and parties. We held dances in the barn. I made huge ranch breakfasts and grand pheasant dinners. Our neighbors taught us about whiskey, and we taught them the little we knew about wine. I spent a great deal of my time at Two Star cooking, cleaning, and hosting. It was an enormous amount of fun and an enormous amount of work.

The year following Two Star's completion, Corrine and her husband asked if I would help them with their summer horse camps for girls. I was honored and actually somewhat surprised they wanted me on their team. Up until that time, I had thought maybe they were just putting up with me because I was Mel's wife and a frequent guest at their ranch. But when they asked me to be part of horse camp, I knew they trusted me as a friend and as a horsewoman. They didn't pay me one cent, and that didn't matter one bit. I was in heaven. Ted and I joined the team.

Corrine and I quickly became close friends. Before Two Star was completed, I had often stayed at Prairie Sky to "audition" horses for our herd or to be nearby for key parts of Two Star's construction. During our many long days and evenings together, we found an easy rapport. Corrine is one of the kindest, truest, funniest people I have ever known. She also "got" what Mel was all about, and she was one of the few people I could speak with honestly about my marriage.

After Ted and I signed on for horse camp, we spent the next three summers with groups of girls ages nine through sixteen for weeklong adventures in riding, camping, and just plain girl fun. While I watched these girls living out their fantasies, I was also living out my own. We rode for hours each day. The girls learned how to saddle up their horses and the basics of barrels and poles in the rodeo arena. We told ghost stories around the campfire. We slept under the stars. We had talent shows and late-night talks about boys.

Every week, we set aside a night to saddle up our horses for a midnight ride under the stars. On hot, dusty afternoons, we washed off our dirt and sweat in local swimming holes. We shared hearty laughs and suffered a few scrapes and spills. We consoled each other during occasional bouts of homesickness, and we celebrated each accomplishment and new experience. Together, and with the help of our wonderful teachers—our very patient horses—we learned how to be better women.

It was during one of these magical summers that my marriage ended.

The Ballroom of Stone

It is difficult to see the truth of your own reality when you are swimming up to your eyeballs in dysfunction—particularly when it rises gradually. Every day in every way, I was disappointing Mel, and I allowed his assessment of me to define my worth. Over time, I learned I was not compliant enough or thin enough or adoring enough to please him.

On any given day, I was either engaged too much or too little in the lives of his three adult children and his two young grandchildren. I was, at turns, too outgoing or too reserved. Either I spent too much time in the garden or not enough. When he decided I was drinking too much wine, I quit. When he decided he missed drinking wine with me, I resumed. I was turning myself inside out to make him happy.

One of Mel's biggest gripes was that I was not "hot" enough. He once told me he thought I was pretty, but he wished I were prettier. He told me prosperous men had hot wives, and as his wife, it was my job to be just that. He wanted me to wear short skirts and low-cut tops. When we went out, he instructed me to "show a lot of leg and a lot of tit." I tended to laugh off these instructions, but I knew he was serious.

Mel purchased clothing for me from catalogs, and most of it was far outside my comfort zone. More often than not, this clothing ended up in the back of my closet, and Mel didn't like that one little bit.

He once took me to a clothing store in Las Vegas and selected several tight and revealing pieces for me to try on. I did my best to be a good sport. I tried it all on and modeled it with flourish, but when I declined to purchase any of it, Mel refused to talk to me for the rest of the day. When he finally broke his silence later that night, it was only to call me an "ungrateful bitch" in the middle of a crowded casino.

Horse camp was pretty much my only break from Mel. There, I knew I was fine just the way I was. I didn't need lipstick or eyeliner or plumped-up breasts or big hair. Jeans, boots, and a ponytail were enough for my campers. There, I was appreciated and loved just because I was me.

Camp ran from Sunday to Friday for four weeks each summer. Corrine and her husband managed the meals and the housekeeping. I, along with two young local women, took care of the girls and the horses.

By the time each camp came to a close on Friday, we

were exhausted. During camp, we worked sixteen-hour days, tending to the needs of our energetic girls. On Friday afternoons, our campers' families returned to Prairie Sky for the final horse show, where the girls had an opportunity to show off what they had learned. By four o'clock, the horse show was over, and we would say our tearful good-byes to the girls. We then cleaned up the barn, released the horses to the pasture, and collapsed in exhaustion on the front porch with a case of beer.

One Friday morning, Mel called me en route from Saint Paul and announced that his friend, Will, was driving up from Rapid City and planned to spend the night with us at Two Star. The prospect was not appealing after a busy week of horse camp, but I voiced no concern and offered to make dinner. When camp wrapped up that afternoon, instead of joining my colleagues for our post-camp debriefing, I hurried back to Two Star to prepare for Mel's and Will's arrivals.

I pulled two pheasants out of the freezer to thaw. I cleaned up the house, changed the sheets in the guest room, and set out towels and a bathrobe for Will. Mel told me he and Will intended to go for a ride before dinner, so I went out to the pasture and brought Ned and Ted up to the barn. I then cleaned myself up as best I could.

Mel and Will soon arrived, saddled up, and took off for their ride. While they were gone, I prepared a beautiful pheasant dinner with all the trimmings. I set out their favorite whiskeys and selected two bottles of wine for our feast. Upon their return, I had cocktails and appetizers waiting for them on the front porch. We enjoyed a fabulous candlelit dinner together. We laughed and told stories and drank every last drop of wine. Despite my exhaustion, it was a fantastic evening.

When we finished dinner, Mel and Will returned to the front porch for whiskey and cigars while I cleaned up the kitchen and started cinnamon rolls for the next day's breakfast. Around eleven o'clock, Mel and Will came back in the house and announced it was time for bed. Will said his goodnights, and Mel joined me in the kitchen. I expected Mel to give me a big hug and a kiss and thank me for putting together such a beautiful evening after a draining week at horse camp. So I was surprised when I looked up and found Mel leaning against the refrigerator, glaring at me.

"What?" I said.

"Will doesn't think you're supportive enough of me, and I agree." He then turned around and went to bed.

I stood there in the silent kitchen for several minutes, surveying my small towers of sparkling clean pots and pans and the rows of cinnamon rolls rising on the counter.

I wasn't angry. I was confused.

I could not understand how the past seven hours— or the past seven years, for that matter—could possibly add up to "unsupportive." On the contrary, I felt that everything I did revolved around supporting Mel.

I thought back over the hundreds of dinners I had cooked for Mel and his family, the countless cocktail parties and business dinners I had hosted and attended, and the birthday parties and holidays I had meticulously planned.

I thought about my tireless support for his work, my willingness to give up my own work, my dedication to our ranch and our Saint Paul home, the love and affection I *thought* I had showered on him, and my daily determination to be the best wife and stepmother I could be. And yet, despite my best intentions, my efforts were somehow perceived as unsupportive.

I rewound through the evening to try to figure out where it went wrong. Nothing stood out to me. I knew, however, that buried somewhere in all the stories, the laughter, and the chatter, some thoughtless and benign comment came out of my mouth that triggered Mel and prompted him to conclude that all my efforts and all my goodwill amounted to a grand total of nothing—and my final grade as his wife was *unsupportive*. Then, he took Will out to the front porch, shared his assessment, and extracted something from Will that Mel read as agreement. By the time Mel returned to the kitchen, it had all been Will's idea and Mel had simply agreed with him.

Over the course of our years together, this scenario had repeated itself more times than I could count, but I kept going back for more. I desperately wanted unconditional love from someone who was completely unequipped to offer it. And while I managed the dysfunction as best I could, day by day I was losing myself.

Even as I became more conscious of the dysfunction in our marriage, my resolve to remain in it did not waver. Never for a moment did I believe our problems were insurmountable, and I was determined to figure out how to fix what was broken between us. I even entertained the notion that I was the problem. Maybe Mel was right. Maybe I was a bitch. Maybe I was undermining him. Maybe there was something deeply wrong with me that was causing all this craziness. I was willing to look at every possibility, except, perhaps, the truth about the person I had married.

During the last six months we were together, Mel's episodes became more and more frequent. Evenings would inevitably end with Mel chastising me for one grave error or another until I was reduced to what he determined to be a satisfactory puddle. He would then go to bed and fall asleep immediately, and I would pour a glass of wine, turn on the TV or open a book, wipe my tears, and fall asleep in the guest room at Two Star or the tiny room in the back of our Saint Paul house. The next morning, Mel would rise cheerfully, kiss me as if nothing had happened, and ask what we were doing for dinner that night.

I felt as if I was going insane.

One morning, after I woke to the usual unsettling

kiss from Mel, I knew I could no longer continue this ridiculous game. Somehow, I found the courage to announce to Mel that I was going to consult a therapist about our issues. I invited Mel to participate, but I made it clear that with or without him, I was going to address matters in therapy. I didn't know how our relationship could be fixed, but I was determined to figure that out. I just needed some help.

Mel elected to participate, probably thinking that his impressive skills as a trial lawyer would enable him to quickly and easily prove to our therapist that there was nothing wrong with our marriage that wasn't attributable to me. Then, I would quit complaining and we could get back to "normal."

Still, I was cautiously optimistic. Soon, however, our weekly sessions devolved into fifty-minute microcosms of our daily lives. Mel yelled. I cried. Our therapist was doing his best, but the dysfunction was proving to be too thick for even him to cut through.

In the summer of 2007, Mel and I had what turned out to be our last counseling session. Our relationship was deteriorating swiftly, and the intensity of our counseling sessions was escalating. As this particularly explosive session neared an end, Mel was so angry, he was shaking. I was scared. I knew that if Mel was this angry with a third party present, it would be much worse when we were alone together.

Thankfully, our therapist also recognized this, and

he made the bold and prudent suggestion that we live separately for a few days for a much-needed cooling-off period. Knowing Mel would never voluntarily leave our house, I suggested that I go home, collect a few things, and spend the night with my friend Barb. Then, as already planned, I would drive to Two Star the next day for the upcoming horse camp, and Mel would go to the Sturgis motorcycle rally with his son, Jay. If additional time was needed after horse camp and the rally ended, I would move temporarily into an empty condo we had on the market for sale. Mel agreed.

As we walked to the elevator after that horrific therapy session, I was sobbing. When we reached the elevator Mel turned to me and very calmly asked what I had planned for dinner that night. I could not believe what I was hearing. It seemed impossible that the man I loved so much could be so cruel, so heartless, and *so clueless* while I was melting into the ground with pain.

When I later considered this complete disconnect between us, I realized that during the six months leading up to that last therapy session, while I had cried enough tears to fill a small ocean, Mel hadn't shed a single tear. He had been going about his business as if nothing was wrong.

Consciously or unconsciously, Mel had created conditions in our marriage that presented me with a very clear choice: either I could morph into the adoring, compliant, hot wife he felt he deserved, or I could leave. If I did the latter, he could move on to a more deserving wife with minimal damage to his reputation. I would be the leaver, and he would be the victim.

The Hospital

The day after that last therapy session, I sullenly drove to Two Star to prepare for the final horse camp of the season. Upon arrival, I checked my email, and I was shocked to learn that almost immediately after we had left the therapist's office, Mel had emailed his parents, my parents, my niece, our siblings, and all his children to announce that I had left him. He solicited their prayers and asked everyone to keep our separation *private*. To the best of my knowledge, no one in the family had any idea Mel and I were having serious problems.

As I closed my inbox, my head was spinning. Once again, my understanding of everything in my life turned inside out. At a time when I did not think I could absorb any more pain, this betrayal struck me like a dagger to my heart that went in one side and out the other. I had witnessed a lot of messed-up stuff during our years together, but I had no idea Mel could hit this far below the belt—particularly when it came to involving my parents.

At the time, my parents were eighty-three and eighty-six years old, and although they'd had some rough years when my sister and I were growing up, they had come a long way with each other since then and they were now happy with each other and extremely supportive of both me and my sister. My parents adored Mel and his family, and although they had seen glimpses of Mel's rage on occasion, they really had no idea anything was seriously wrong in our marriage. The fact that Mel would drag my parents into this mess without warning enraged me. His complete lack of empathy for me and our family members was unfathomable.

I immediately called my parents. Thankfully, they had not yet read Mel's email. I did the best I could to explain what had happened. As always, they were rock solid with their support. They were clearly confused and concerned, but they assured me they would be able to manage their own pain and disappointment. They encouraged me to focus my energy on taking care of myself. I then went out to Two Star's front porch and cried my heart out. There did not seem to be any possible way we could piece our relationship back together. Mel's email had destroyed whatever tenuous trust remained between us.

Somehow, I managed to drag myself out of bed the next morning. Horse camp began as usual, and I did what I had to do with the girls, but I felt dead inside. I no longer recognized my own life. It was not only the agony of Mel's betrayal, but also the painful reality that life as I knew it was over.

Realistically, I knew that I could not maintain Two Star on my own and that Mel would end up taking all of it from me, but emotionally, such a future was nearly impossible to grasp. Despite the hell I had been through the past several months, it had never once occurred to me that I would not grow old teaching girls to ride on those five hundred acres of prairie. Tears welled up in my eyes from time to time, but I managed to soldier on.

Every time I patted Ted or hugged a girl or took in a beautiful vista, I knew it could very well be the last time. Over the years, every piece of that prairie had imprinted itself on my mind and my heart, and minute by minute and hour by hour, I silently said good-bye to all of it.

I told Corrine an abbreviated version of what had happened. She was clearly heartbroken, but I could tell she wasn't surprised. Much like my parents, Corrine would be a tiger in the trees for me, and I knew I could rely on her for help and protection as I struggled to make sense of my future. She looked deep into my eyes and said, "Don't forget how strong you are." I didn't feel strong by any measure, but I knew I would have to find strength to get through this.

I didn't tell anyone else at camp about recent events, but I expect they knew something was up. Corrine had probably told them to carry on, not ask me any questions, and just let me be.

Difficult as those days were, having horse camp to distract me was a blessing. Someone once said, "There is nothing better for the inside of a person than the outside of a horse." I never believed that more than I did when I was with Ted those first days after my separation from Mel. Ted, Corrine, and camp kept me from crumbling.

Then on the third day of horse camp, I was called to the house for a phone call. I picked up the phone and was surprised to hear Mel's twenty-seven-year-old son, Jay, on the other end. He had some news. Jay and Mel had been on their way to the rally in Sturgis. Several miles out of Pierre, South Dakota, they had an accident. Mel was driving too fast over a hill and was unable to stop his motorcycle in time to avoid a road construction barrier. He was not critically hurt, but he was in the hospital, and Jay asked me if I would come.

Pierre was a four-hour drive from the ranch. I quickly threw a few things in a bag and told Corrine I had to leave camp immediately. I briefly explained what had happened. Despite her concern for Mel, Corrine smiled and drew me into her arms. She and I both had the same conviction: this was God's way of bringing Mel and me back together. The timing was just too remarkable to believe otherwise. I was nervous and scared, but I was filled with hope as I sped away, still wearing my dirty ranch clothes from the morning.

As I drove down the driveway from Prairie Sky, I caught sight of Ted in my rearview mirror. He was tied up in front of the barn, still saddled and sweaty from the morning ride. As he watched me drive away, I noticed that his ears were uncharacteristically pinned back against his head. I didn't know that this would be the last time I would see him—but I think he did.

When I arrived at the hospital, I embraced Jay. He looked as if he had been through hell. Not only had he seen his dad take a terrible fall, but he now faced the prospect of spending his long-awaited vacation in a hospital.

Mel was in rough shape, but he was stable. When I entered his room, he was fully sedated and sleeping peacefully. The hospital staff explained that he had a few minor injuries, one of which would require him to remain in the hospital as long as needed for it to heal. I spent the rest of the evening talking with staff, signing papers, and making telephone calls to the people who needed to know about the accident.

Although Jay certainly knew some of what had happened between Mel and me (at least Mel's version of events), he and I were happy hospital companions. We kept each other amused, took turns sitting vigil with Mel, and encouraged each other to sleep and eat. I had known this kid for a long time, and I was happy to be there with him. Being around Jay and Mel gave me comfort and hope.

Jay checked in to a hotel, and I gathered up a few blankets and pillows and made a makeshift bed on the floor in Mel's room. I refused to leave his side. The first few nights, Mel woke numerous times in a semiconscious state, often trying to pull his IV out of his arm and get out of bed. I rarely slept, but I could not be persuaded to leave his room. A few nights in, a kind nurse brought in a small mattress for me. I enjoyed one blissful night of comfort before the fire marshal declared the mattress a hazard and I had to go back to the hard linoleum. All told, I spent ten nights on that floor.

A day or two after the accident, other family members started to arrive in Pierre. Although they initially seemed happy to see me, it soon became clear they had their own idea of how this whole hospital thing was going to work. Of course, they had all been on Mel's email list, so they knew something had happened between us.

I made a few lame attempts to explain what had been going on with me and Mel, but it really wasn't the time or the place to sort out the details of our troubled marriage, so we all just let that issue remain the elephant in the room. We just focused on Mel and managed the awkwardness as best we could.

A few days later, however, I noticed that the tone of our "solidarity" began to change. The doctors and nurses were talking to Mel's family about his condition rather than to me. His family started fielding the telephone calls coming in from concerned relatives and friends. One day, needing the phone number of one of Mel's friends, I opened his locker and could not locate his phone. I asked a nurse where it was, and she told me

Mel's sister had taken it. I then noticed that his watch and wedding ring were also missing. When I asked about them, the nurse told me Mel's sister had taken those too. Clearly, the rules had changed.

While Mel recovered and returned to consciousness, his family, including Jay, gathered in secretive huddles in the hallways and lounges. When I asked about their plans, they smiled and told me they had none. They rarely even spoke to me. They moved together as a group, but always left at least one of them in the room with Mel and me. I had absolutely no idea how long they intended to stay in Pierre or what they had in mind for Mel after his discharge, but I knew they had a plan.

I left the hospital for only an hour each day to buy food and supplies. Pierre is a small town, so my breaks usually involved a trip to Walmart. I bought a small lamp so I could read on the floor in the evenings. The only private time I had with my husband was after his family left for their restaurant dinners and comfy hotel rooms. By then, Mel was asleep, so I read or did crossword puzzles until I could no longer stay awake. I then plumped up my blankets and pillows and fell asleep on that hard, unforgiving floor. I felt completely and utterly alone.

As the sleepless days and nights continued, I began to deteriorate physically and emotionally. Having few clothes and very little else with me, I began to look increasingly disheveled. I was often tearful. The hospital staff, although always polite, started to treat me like the forlorn being I was becoming. As Mel's family cooled to my presence, the hospital staff started doing the same.

The Bradys charmed the staff with their jokes and folksy good humor, and with their coaching, I am certain the hospital staff decided I was the "bad guy" in this scenario. I was the ungrateful wife who left her sweet, adoring husband and his wonderful family. I knew Mel's family well enough to know how they operated when it came to protecting their own. Everyone around me was in the same happy, helpful club, while I slept on the floor in the corner like a loyal but neglected dog.

Mel's family eventually told me they would allow me to take care of Mel when he returned home to Saint Paul. This was something I wanted to do anyway, but I was not the decision maker here. I was also not consulted on the logistics of getting Mel back home. I was the only one in Pierre who had a car. Everyone else had flown in. But with his injuries only tenuously healed, I knew it would not be possible for Mel to join me on the seven-hour drive back to Saint Paul.

I had no idea what the Bradys were planning until the hospital arranged a discharge meeting in Mel's room two days before he was to leave. While we all sat in chairs in a semicircle around Mel's bed, the nurses and other medical staff explained what Mel would need when he returned home. A nurse asked who would be his primary caregiver. I raised my hand.

Although Mel had previously consented to this

arrangement, as soon as my hand went up, Mel flew into a rage—his first at the hospital in the presence of others. Mel spoke forcefully and belligerently, covering several topics, including, but not limited to, his certainty that I would try to kill him, that I was stealing money from him, and that my friends were cheating whores who were plotting against him.

In all fairness to Mel, he may well have been feeling the effects of medication. The most surreal part of the episode, however, was his family's reaction. As Mel ranted, his family remained completely calm and impassive. While Mel continued and his family failed to intervene or respond, one by one the hospital staff widened their eyes. They looked from Mel to me to the family and soon realized their prior assessment of the situation had been dead wrong. I could see the apology in their eyes, and for one brief, shining moment, I felt that someone else had seen the reality that was my life. It was a relief to feel even this small bit of validation, but it did not change a single thing.

Mel's rage made it clear to everyone that I could not take care of him during his recovery. It would not be healthy for him, and it would not be healthy for me. The hospital episode was now over—and so were any chances of reconciliation.

While Mel's family completed their arrangements for a private plane to take Mel back to Saint Paul, I quietly left the hospital and drove home to Minnesota. I gave up any illusion that the accident was going to heal what was broken between us. The entire ordeal felt like a cruel joke.

And Then
She Was Happy

When I got back to our Saint Paul house, my animal companions, Henry and Prickly Pete, met me at the door. While Mel was in the hospital, friends had driven them from Two Star to Saint Paul and taken care of them while I was gone. It was the first time in a long time that somebody other than a Walmart greeter was happy to see me.

Several years earlier, I had adopted Henry from a rescue group. Henry is a big, lumbering Airedale terrier who spent his early years as a breeding dog, living in squalor at a puppy mill in Iowa. Henry would not win any academic awards at Canine College, but he is one hundred pounds of pure unconditional love. Like Ted, Henry protects me.

Prickly Pete was Two Star's barn cat, and she pretty much ran the show on the five hundred acres of prairie she patrolled. She is a sweet, loving gray tabby, but it was her prowess as a hunter that earned her the title Director of Wildlife Management in South Dakota. Mel hated cats, and there was no possible way I was going to leave her behind. So now, she too would have to adjust to a new life in Saint Paul.

After I got the house in order, I packed up some clothes, a set of towels, and some sheets. Still feeling caught under Mel's possessive thumb, I was reluctant to remove even the most basic things from the house.

I then loaded up Henry and Prickly Pete and drove to Target to buy some essentials. These included one knife, one fork, one spoon, one water glass, some take-out food, a few pet supplies, and a twelve-pack of Diet Coke. The three of us then drove to our new home—a condominium on the edge of downtown Saint Paul that contained little more than an old mattress on the bed-room floor. I had owned this condo before Mel and I married, and we had maintained it as a rental property during our marriage. After our last renter had moved out several months earlier, we had decided to put it on the market. I now realized that the timing of this deci-sion could not have been better.

When we arrived at the condo, I cracked open a Diet Coke, set up the litter box, and sat down on the liv-ing room floor. Our last tenant had left some firewood next to the fireplace, so I made a small fire.

This was the first time in weeks that I had had a

moment to take a breath. I was physically and emotionally exhausted. I sat back against the wall and looked around at the bare space. I rested my hand on Henry's back and watched Prickly Pete silently explore her new home.

I waited for the full weight of my losses to come crashing down around me. I knew it was coming. Finally, the moment had arrived when I had a chance to process all that had happened, all I had lost, and all I had left behind. I expected to hear, in Lorrie Moore's words, everything I had given and everything I had sacrificed fall to the floor with a loud clunk. I was now in a quiet place where I could feel the true gravity of my situation, and I was prepared for the worst.

But there, in the silence of that empty room, only one thought entered my mind. It was very different from what I expected, and it came to me loud, clear, and unequivocal. It was this: *I am so happy.*

And I truly did feel happy for the first time in a very long time. Through all the chaos of those past few weeks, I had felt little more than panic, anger, and fear. There had been no time to process, no time to feel—no time to just be with myself.

Over the years of our marriage, I had allowed Kristi to slowly fade away. Now, in this quiet, empty condo, I felt what it was like to be back with her, out of that dark Saint Paul house and that pretty little ranch that had turned from a place of joy to a place of devastating pain. I finally had some distance from Mel's judgments and his over-bearing family—and unexpected as it was, I felt happy.

Although it may have seemed as if I had lost every-thing, this was actually the point my life began-or, per-haps more accurately, resumed. At the age of fifty, I felt a deep and true joy that I had not known for many, many years.

On that cool fall evening on the condo floor, with my knife, my fork, and my spoon, and with my pets sitting watch over me, I began my journey back to self-respect. I was on the road to self-recovery. That is, I started to recover *myself.* I started to heal.

Lawyering Up

Soon the legal proceedings for our divorce began. When the time came to get an attorney on board, I quickly learned I could not hire my former firm to represent me. Mel had used them for his first divorce prior to my working there. Now, without his consent, the conflict of interest simply could not be overcome.

So I did what I believed to be the next best thing: I hired a woman I did not know personally, but who was considered one of the very best family law attorneys in Minnesota. When I called her office to request a consultation, her assistant barely took a breath before announcing that she charged $450 an hour and required a $10,000 retainer.

Sure, whatever, I thought. I could figure out how to do that. But it struck me as strange that they would treat a potential client so brusquely. The message was clear: *You need us more than we need you.* Although very different from how my former firm operated, I thought they knew what they were doing, and so I went along with the program.

At our first substantive meeting, my attorney made it crystal clear that she didn't give a rat's ass about what I had been through. She had spoken with Mel's attorney before this meeting, so she had some information about our situation. When I started to tell her my story, she put up her hand and said, "I don't need to hear that." She went on to say that from what she understood, Mel felt very hurt and betrayed by the fact that I had left him and I needed to be sensitive to that as we moved forward.

Say *what*? It was as if I was walking around with a "kick me" sign on my back. But did I turn around and leave her office? No.

My gut was telling me loud and clear that this professional relationship was not going to work. I expected and needed to work with someone who would listen to me, offer me support, and be on my side. I did not expect her to be my confidante, my therapist, or anything other than an advocate, but I *did* expect to be respected and heard. I felt the disconnect from the very beginning, but I said nothing about it and kept working with her until the divorce was final—nearly two years and a big chunk of money later. I trusted her reputation more than I trusted myself. If *anyone* should have known better, it was me.

I now know what it feels like to walk into an attorney's office, feeling desperately lost and alone, and how deeply disappointing it is not to feel heard by the one person who *should* be there for you. It was another heartbreaking lesson in not trusting my gut, not asking for what I needed, and then ending up feeling victimized.

And this was not my attorney's fault. It was mine. I have no doubt that my attorney is a good person and a gifted professional. I did not give her an opportunity to give me what I needed because I never asked her for it.

After reflecting on all that had happened—my marriage and separation, the hospital, and my relationship with my attorney—I began to notice how easily I fell into the role of *victim*. It was not a comfortable role, but I soon realized it was a familiar one. Growing up, I had often felt like a victim in my family. My parents were frequently at odds, my sister was emotionally absent, and I was working my ass off trying to make us a happy family (something which eventually did happen, but not until long after I entered adulthood).

Early in my childhood, I learned that my needs were not important. I didn't feel seen or heard by anyone. Not being seen and heard was a slow-building and subtle form of trauma. It was like taking a little drop of poison every day, and over time, it built up in me. I carried that poison around in me for most of my adult life. I have no doubt that I chose Mel as my partner because the dynamic of our relationship was so familiar to me. And then, at the age of fifty and facing a divorce, I chose as my ally an attorney who perfectly mirrored my family and my marriage.

Old familiar patterns were rearing their heads with merciless persistence, and I finally started to take notice of that. I started to pay attention to the choices I was making. I began to sit at the feet of my own life and allow it to teach me.

Moving Forward

That unexpectedly peaceful first night at the condo marked the first step in disengaging from my marriage and building an entirely new life. The pain from my marriage and all I had lost along with it was still very fresh, but physically removing myself from the situation gave me a great deal of peace. Although I was sleeping on a mattress on a floor 450 miles from our beloved ranch, I was able to live through an entire day without being criticized and without being demeaned—and that alone was wonderful.

After I was settled in the condo (which took about fifteen minutes), I started considering my options for the future. I had no furniture, little in the way of kitchen and household supplies, no job prospects, and a burning desire to start over.

While in South Dakota, I had enrolled in an online veterinary technology program in an effort to make myself more useful with our horses and our neighbors' animals. Now on my own, I considered finishing my certification, but it just didn't make sense to invest an additional $20,000 to complete a degree that would yield me little more than that in annual income.

And, of course, I had a law degree. I had to consider that. My memories of law practice were clouded by that last year when I was battling rheumatoid arthritis. The pain at that time was such a powerful distraction that I was not able to enjoy my work at all. But aside from those painful memories, there was much that I did love about practicing law. It was at least worth a shot to see if I could do something satisfying with my law degree and still maintain my health.

Because of my disability, my attorney license was inactive, and in order to reactivate it, I had to earn ninety continuing-education credits. I wanted to start working some sort of job immediately, but I needed a flexible schedule so I would have time to take the necessary law classes over the next eight to ten months. I chose part-time work at a downtown Saint Paul department store, thinking the employee discount would provide value to me beyond the $8 an hour I would earn selling clothing in the children's department. So I joined the retail workforce.

It was not an enjoyable job. Often it was downright depressing. But day in and day out, I did what I had to do to be a good employee. I was always on time and remained productive for the twenty or so hours I was offered each week. I made friends with my coworkers, won a few customer service awards (receiving $5 for each), and found a kind of Zen pleasure in organizing clothing racks. I earned my meager paychecks, started accumulating household supplies, and felt some measure of satisfaction purchasing deeply discounted children's clothing for my friends' kids. It wasn't joy galore, but it was a start.

The part-time retail work gave me the flexibility I needed to complete my continuing-education classes, and within ten months I had reactivated my attorney license. I also sold the condo, used the proceeds to purchase a pretty little house in an old Saint Paul neighborhood, and parlayed my employee discount at the department store into a houseful of furniture and kitchen supplies. Savings and a line of credit kept me afloat while the divorce slowly moved forward.

Without much in the way of intention, I moved in the direction of starting my own law practice. Although a home office wasn't in my mind when I purchased my house, it turned out to be an ideal place to test the waters of solo practice. My house had two small rooms and a bathroom that were largely separate from the rest of the house. There I created a home office and a meeting room.

I had been doing some reading on feng shui (the practice of arranging space to facilitate the flow of positive energy), and I asked a feng shui practitioner to help me arrange my home and business space. I took down one small wall to create the workable flow she suggested. Because the entire first floor of the house had to be repainted, she suggested that I write words on the walls of each room to embody my intention for each space.

When the painters arrived, they were surprised to find words primitively painted on the walls of each room. My home office announced itself as a space for *prosperity*, *energy*, and *excellence*. My meeting room was a place of *truth*, *healing*, and *compassion*. The dining room was a place of *love*, *family*, and *togetherness*. And so it went throughout my house.

When I look back on all of this, I am amazed and, quite honestly, impressed at what I managed to accomplish during that period when my divorce was pending and my law practice had yet to reemerge. I had no idea where all this would take me. All I knew was that I had to take one step at a time in the direction that felt truest and trust that the universe would take me where I needed to go.

So that's what I did. I did not impose any expectations on myself, other than to do something every day that would move me forward. Sometimes it was something big like tearing down a wall. Sometimes it was nothing more than moving a box. All I asked of myself was to do *something*. And this included doing things to take care of myself.

Yoga became a huge part of my self-care. In what I believe to be an act of divine providence, I attended my first yoga class shortly before my marriage imploded. Yoga found me at exactly the right time.

During the first four decades of my life, I had been very physically active. Before entering law school, I was a physical education teacher. I was also a high school athlete and a fitness trainer. I was dedicated to regular exercise long before it became fashionable. But when arthritis struck in my early forties, my fitness regimen took a backseat to pain management. Even after starting on the medication that essentially eradicated my pain, I did not resume any kind of regular exercise. I was the embodiment of Newton's law: a body in motion tends to stay in motion; a body at rest tends to stay at rest.

This started to change when I attended my first yoga class shortly before my fiftieth birthday. I was immediately hooked. I started to practice nearly every day, and I continue to do so. I truly believe yoga is the best single thing I do in my life. Yoga takes me to a place where I let go of control and expectation. It helps me reconnect with my best self in body, mind, and soul, and it teaches me to believe—truly believe—that my life is exactly the way it is supposed to be.

During this time of enormous transition, I started to embrace other opportunities I would have otherwise deferred or dismissed. I opened myself up to whatever classes, seminars, or retreats crossed my path. When something interesting came along, I asked myself three questions:

1. Do I want to do this?

2. Can I fit it in my schedule?

3. Can I afford it?

If the answer to all three was yes, I would ask myself one more question: Why *wouldn't* I? If I didn't have a good response to that last question, I did it.

So it came to be that I had some pretty nice experiences—all of which contributed in big and small ways to my healing. I took classes in everything from meditation and energy healing to financial planning. I read lots of books. I went on retreats. I got regular massages. I spent time with my friends and my neighbor kids and my animals. I practiced yoga religiously. In sum, while I was doing my best to get myself back on my feet financially and professionally, I was also doing my best to take care of myself.

Very few, if any, of these experiences were profound. There were no grand "aha moments" or major emotional breakthroughs. Everything was cumulative. I simply stayed mindful of the choices I made every day, and I allowed these choices—every class, every walk with Henry, and every evening on the couch watching TV with my neighbor kids—to ground and support me emotionally and spiritually, and together it all moved me in a positive direction. I rebuilt my life day by day, minute by minute, drop by drop.

Some of these experiences required money, but many of them cost nothing more than a small investment of time and a short drive or bike ride. I attended a free two-hour introductory meditation class a few blocks from my home. There I reconnected with a woman I had clerked with when I was in law school—more than fifteen years earlier. We are now close friends and valued colleagues. Our offices are literally next door to each other.

I took another class a few blocks in the other direction. There I met a young woman who was training to be an energy healer. She offered her services to me at no cost because she needed practice and I needed healing. She also introduced me to a woman who was training to do Thai massage. She became a dear friend and offered her services to me for a nominal fee. In turn, I helped her incorporate her business. I started to see that there were no limits to what was out there for me. I just had to open myself up to the possibilities and make room for them in my life.

The pain of my losses stirred fairly frequently. I missed Ted and Ned and Two Star every day, and I continued to struggle with robust feelings of anger and betrayal toward Mel. But rather than avoiding or suppressing the pain, I just let it be and I managed it as best I could. Bedtime tended to be difficult, so I created a new ritual. Before I went to bed, I lit a candle to honor my pain and put on a CD of ancient Chinese chanting believed to facilitate healing. I fell asleep to that chanting every night for many, many months. It didn't eliminate my pain, but it helped.

Throughout the long process of getting divorced, starting my new law practice, and moving into my new home, I made a conscious decision not to worry. Good intentions aside, however, worry continued to knock at my door. Those many times when I woke up in the middle of the night—anxious about whether I would be able to make the next month's mortgage payment or succeed as an attorney or be able to manage any of the other worries that vied for my attention—I very intentionally decided not to succumb to worry. I knew worrying was not helpful to me in any way and that the energy it required was much better invested elsewhere. It took practice to put worry aside, but I learned how to do it.

Several months before the divorce was final and only a week or two after my law license was renewed, I was enjoying a beautiful summer evening, eating sushi and drinking wine on my front porch with my friend Rob. The phone rang. It was Mel. I didn't normally accept calls from him, but I was expecting another call, and I picked up the phone without thinking. The topic of that evening's call was *How Are You Going to Support Yourself? Because I Am Not Going To.*

Mellowed by the wine and buoyed by a lovely

evening, I patiently told Mel that my law license had reactivated and that I was moving in the direction of a solo practice. Apparently, Mel found this tremendously amusing: "Are you kidding me? You will *never* pull that off. Where do you think *you* are going to find clients? You are delusional. You do not have what it takes to make this work." I think he might have added, "You can't handle the truth!"

When he finished, I said, "Well, Mel, I expect that when you started your solo practice, people told you that you wouldn't be able to make it work, but you managed to do it."

In a volume easily overheard by Rob, Mel shouted into the phone, "You are *dead wrong*, little lady. Nobody said that to me, because *I* am Mel Brady—and *you*, my dear, are no Mel Brady!"

Beside me on the porch, Rob looked alarmed. I smiled, covered the phone, and whispered, "Welcome to my world." The call soon ended, and surprisingly enough, I took nothing of what Mel said to heart. I knew I had a rough road ahead of me, but I also knew I was moving in the right direction—and Mel had absolutely nothing to say about that. This was the first time Mel wasn't able to "hook" me. And that was that. I knew I was free.

Enough

Enough encompasses both limits and abundance. For me, the limit was getting to the point where I'd had enough of the pain and dysfunction in my marriage. The abundance was getting to the other side with a divorce settlement that was fair—not too little, not too much—just enough.

I knew that by saying "enough" to Mel, I was taking a huge risk. There were a lot of really good things in my life with him, and it was terrifying to think about losing them. But when the pain got to the point where it simply could no longer be ignored, I had a choice: I could stuff the pain inside me and protect what I had—or I could take a big risk, trust my gut, tell the truth, and let the chips fall where they may. I knew that if I chose the former, my true self would gradually evaporate and eventually disappear altogether. If I did the latter, I could lose everything I thought was important—my marriage, my security, our ranch, and my life as I knew it.

I chose the latter. I had reached the point where I was willing to put all those "good" things on the line, so that I could live an authentic life. When I finally said "enough," I did so with every hope that Mel would wake up, come to the table, and work with me to make things better. I had faith in Mel, and I had faith in our marriage. Sadly, this did not happen. Now I had another choice: I could either walk back into the dysfunction, morph into the wife Mel wanted, and allow myself to disappear—or I could take a bold step forward into the unknown.

I thank God every day for giving me the clarity I needed to make the choice I did. Somewhere deep inside, I found the strength to say yes to an authentic self I hardly even remembered and to continue down the path that would bring me back to her.

As the divorce slowly progressed, and as I moved forward step by step into a very new life, I next had to decide *how* I would leave the marriage. It was a long and arduous process, and although I managed to keep myself as insulated as possible from Mel's toxicity, it was difficult to make reasoned decisions when anger and betrayal were still so fresh.

Because we did not have children together, all of the issues in our divorce were financial. This meant we had to value what we had, separate what we each owned before our marriage (called non-marital property), and divide the remainder equitably. Owning two homes and all that went along with them, Mel and I had a lot of possessions. Mel liked stuff, and he wanted to keep all of it. Some of these things were painful to lose (particularly Ted and Ned and Two Star), but by this time, it all carried with it an aura of pain I no longer wanted in my life. So Mel kept about 99.9 percent of our possessions.

I kept my trusty car, a few pieces of jewelry I didn't much like, a set of dishes from my parents, and a few small paintings. Mel kept everything else: the house, the motorcycles, the horses, the ranch, the land, the art, all our furnishings and ranch equipment, the horse trailer, the ATV—pretty much everything. He even kept the beautiful piano he had given me as a wedding gift. He didn't know how to play it, but he was possessive, and I did not have the strength to fight for it.

Although it was difficult to lose some of those things and come to terms with saying good-bye in my heart to Ned and Ted, my piano, and our beautiful little ranch, in the end I knew these things would end up being more of a burden than a blessing. Although I had concerns about Mel's ability to properly care for our horses, I knew they were tough, and I wanted them to stay together in South Dakota.

It was heartbreaking to leave everything behind, but all I really wanted or needed was "enough." And that's what I got. I got enough money to launch a new life for myself and create some financial stability for my future. I got a pretty little house I adore, and I got Henry and Prickly Pete to a happy home. But the best thing I got was freedom and a chance to reconnect with a really cool person I hadn't known for a long time—me.

I soon realized that the only stuff I really needed was a knife, a fork, a spoon, and a safe place to rest my head with Henry and Prickly Pete. The places and animals and possessions I cherished would live in my heart forever, and that would have to be enough. I made good choices, and although it hurts to reminisce about the ranch and the life I left in South Dakota, I honestly have no regrets. Enough is enough.

And Then She Went Back to Work

Soon my practice was launched. When the phone started ringing for my professional services, however, I found myself withering with fear. My instinct was to refer potential clients elsewhere, but I managed to resist the urge to flee from the work.

After nearly eight years away from my law practice, I did not know if I would be able to do it again. As I took on my first clients, I started to realize how many things had changed in the arena of family law. Yes, I had taken ninety credits of continuing-education classes, but the family law courses were hit and miss. I didn't get much in the way of substantive re-education until I started doing the work.

The thought of relearning everything was daunting, but rather than allowing this to overwhelm me, I decided to accept the fact that it would be impossible to learn everything at once. All I could do was figure out the case in front of me. And day by day, client by client, I did just that.

Before my home office was up and running, my first client gave me a $500 retainer in cash at a Starbucks and asked me to help him with a difficult custody matter involving his son. I was terrified. This hardworking, earnest young man was entrusting me with the most important relationship in his life. I humbly accepted the work and deposited the money in my newly established—and aptly named—trust account. I didn't have much in the way of confidence yet, but I got to work.

I had no business plan and I did no marketing other than a website, but people found me. It started slowly, with a few referrals I nervously took on. I was afraid I would not have the smarts or the motivation to make this work. Self-doubt could easily have consumed me, but somehow I managed to keep it at bay, and I just kept moving forward. Rather than having a receptionist and a paralegal taking care of all the details, I figured out how to do most tasks by myself, outsourcing only my bookkeeping and technical support.

And despite Mel's prediction, I *did* pull it off. I wasn't making the kind of income I would have made at a big firm, but I was living and working on my own terms. I soon realized that being a sole practitioner was a perfect fit for me. Although I had loved my work at the firm, I had often felt like a caged animal. Just getting into my office every morning—fighting the traffic, the weather, and the pantyhose—was exhausting. By the time I got home at night, I sometimes felt I had been through a small war. Now, I had the opportunity to create the kind of practice that best suited me. It was not a selfish choice; it was an authentic choice.

Early on, I was concerned that clients would find my home-based practice unprofessional. But I soon learned that clients loved my house with its stress-free atmosphere and easy parking. Henry and Prickly Pete took naturally to their unexpected roles as therapy animals, often offering a nudge or a sweet purr when broken people needed it most. It was good and it was right. I was back on my path, and I was doing the best work of my life.

My new practice was different not only in form but also in function, because I was different. My work was coming from a different place in myself. I had always taken my role as a legal technician very seriously, and I knew I was good at it. But now, I started seeing that technical proficiency was only one measure of what a truly effective family law attorney can offer his or her clients.

Having been through the divorce process myself, I had a new awareness of the needs of the "whole client," and this transformed my practice. My own divorce had given me a new perspective on my clients' pain. They knew I was on the journey with them—both as an attorney and as a fellow traveler.

As my practice steadily grew, the day eventually arrived when I knew I could not take on one more client. I had to figure out the next step. To other business owners, the natural choice may have been to focus on expansion, and I seriously considered adding support staff and recruiting additional attorneys. But I knew in my heart that I did not want to focus my professional life on running a business. I wanted to spend my time helping my clients. Perhaps the day would come when there would be a way for me to help more people, but for the time being, I was happy where I was and with what I could accomplish on my own.

Now, I had the painful luxury of choosing the people I wanted to work with. I provided a free consultation to nearly anyone who asked, but I made it clear that I accepted only a limited number of clients. It was important that the clients I took on got the time and attention they deserved. I also did not want to work myself into the ground. It had to be a good fit for my clients and a good fit for me.

Potential clients who were too consumed with their own anger and pain to make healthy choices for themselves and their families were referred to other competent attorneys. I chose to work with men and women who were not afraid to see their own blind spots, who deep in their hearts wanted to do the right thing, and who trusted me and gave me the benefit of the doubt as we made the tactical decisions necessary to get them where they wanted to be.

Without the added financial stressors of a large staff and overhead, I was able to offer my services at a much lower cost than I would have been able to offer at a firm. This allowed me to work with the people I was passionate about helping: middle-class working families who did not have the resources or the inclination to engage in protracted and expensive divorce proceedings.

At my former firm, I had the privilege of working with professional athletes and business leaders, whose complex family and financial interests gave me great training. But these were not the people I felt called to serve. I knew my gifts were better utilized elsewhere. On those occasions when complex marital estates present themselves, I happily refer these people to my former firm, and I know they will be treated well.

Being true to myself and allowing the universe to take me where I need to go has brought me the most satisfying work I can imagine. This is not to say it is easy. I get tired, agitated, and frustrated more often than I would like to admit. Sometimes, the choices people make during the process of uncoupling are downright depressing. I experience inspiring highs and deflating lows, but through it all, I know I am doing exactly what I should be doing—at least for now.

Miraval

A year and a half after I launched my practice, I was sitting at my desk one day, and I felt tired. Really tired. My divorce had been final for more than a year, my practice had grown to the point where I was able to relocate to a nearby office building, and I had recently completed a rigorous, year-long professional coaching program. My life was relatively stable, and I was tired. As I sat back in my chair, I realized I had not taken a trip unrelated to professional training or wifely duties in many, many years. It was time.

I could afford only a short break, so I thought back over all the places and experiences I had stored up for "someday." I spent some time on the Internet and soon found myself signing up for a long weekend at Miraval, a wellness resort in the foothills of the Santa Catalina Mountains outside of Tucson, Arizona. I cashed in some aging frequent flyer miles, scored a good summer deal at Miraval, and prepared for my first *real* vacation in what felt like eons.

I arrived at Miraval on a Friday afternoon, well prepared for my three-night visit. I had carefully studied the resort's online materials and selected the activities and classes that interested me. My first organized activity would take place the next morning, so on Friday I simply allowed myself to melt into blissful solitude in the beautiful place that is Miraval.

Saturday morning I woke early, excited to attend to my plans for the day. First on the agenda was the challenge course, which consists of a collection of ropes and poles scattered throughout a few acres in the desert. The challenge I had chosen was called Quantum Leap Two.

"QL-II," as it is known to veterans, is a partnered activity in which teams of two take turns climbing up a thirty-five-foot telephone pole embedded in the desert floor. Small hand and foot pegs are affixed to the pole to assist with the climb. Once at the top, the first team member climbs on top of a platform about the size of a cookie sheet without anything other than the pole and their self-confidence to hold onto. Throughout, the pole moves a bit from side to side to accommodate the wind and frequent weight shifts.

The other team member then makes the climb and, with any luck, joins the first on the cookie sheet. Once settled, the climbers share supportive looks, join hands, look out at the desert, and then joyously leap off the pole into the safety of their harnesses. They are then lowered to the ground, where they celebrate their strength and courage and proceed to lunch and the spa. It sounded easy enough.

I expected that the physical aspects of the challenge would be mild to accommodate Miraval's largely middle-aged clientele, and I thought the lessons learned would be valuable, but not profound. I also expected that I would excel at every single part of it. I jumped out of bed, ready to dive in. I brushed my teeth, threw on a T-shirt and shorts, and headed out into the beautiful Arizona sun for my day of peace and joy. That damn pole, however, had something very different in mind for me.

As the group gathered, we chose our partners. My partner was an annoyingly fit anesthesiologist from a Tennessee university. As we walked the path to the challenge course with our facilitator and group of eight, my partner and I spoke with easy anticipation about the challenge ahead, the beautiful weather, and our plans for the day.

We arrived at the challenge course and received our instructions. We then climbed into our harnesses and chose the order in which we would climb. My high-achieving partner volunteered to go first. This meant I would be second. Sounded good to me.

My partner approached the pole confidently and quickly began her ascent. About twenty feet off the ground, however, her confidence waned and her body started shaking. Soon, she froze entirely. Her short breaths were audible to us below. "I don't think I can do this," she whispered. I was really surprised this woman turned out to be so lame.

But after much encouragement from the group and with great determination, she managed to coax one foot above the other, and she bravely continued up the pole. As she neared the top, the shaking resumed, and she burst into tears. "I don't want to die," she cried.

Between sobs, she told the group that she had no confidence in the ropes and harnesses, and she doubted the competence of the other group members who were on belay and responsible for lowering her back to the ground. All her fears and doubts were externally focused. She trusted herself completely. She simply did not trust other people to keep her safe.

But she did not give up. She hung in there with herself, and she managed to get herself to the top of the pole. Her tears continued, but she eventually found stable footing on the cookie sheet. It was clear that she was not going to let her fear hold her back.

Now it was my turn. I began confidently, wanting to show the rest of the group how this was supposed to be done. The first few steps were fine. Soon, however, and much to my surprise, halfway up the pole I, too, froze. It was a kind of panic I had never experienced so viscerally. It permeated every cell in my body, and I burst into tears.

Although I was unaware of much besides my own terror, I do remember being completely shocked that this had happened. I had had absolutely no doubt that I would be able to climb up that stupid pole. Unlike my partner, however, my fear was not about the harness or the ropes or the group members on belay. I had complete trust in all things external. What I did not trust was myself. I did not believe my body could get me up that pole.

I remained on the pole for several minutes, considering my options. None of them had any appeal. I could not imagine continuing up, and I was afraid of what would happen if I let go. I finally realized I had to do something. Staying there indefinitely was not an option. Eventually, I found the courage to let go, and I allowed the team to lower me safely to the ground.

I felt like the biggest loser on earth.

My partner, now relatively comfortable on the platform, had regained her composure, but she now had to face the reality that what goes up must come down. After a fair amount of encouragement from the group, she jumped off the pole and made a soft landing with the help of the team. Her return to solid ground was accompanied by cheers from the group and the joy of having accomplished something amazing.

I joined the celebration for her and the other six brave souls who took on the pole that morning, but I felt as if I had been hit by a bus I never saw coming. It had never occurred to me that I would not be able to complete this challenge. It was just another task on my agenda. Yet, I could not do it.

With the challenge completed, the group walked back to the resort. I said my good-byes with the best grace and good humor I could muster, but instead of resuming my day with lunch and spa, I marched directly to the Miraval bookstore to find a book that would help me address the fear and self-doubt that had seemingly come out of nowhere and smacked me down from that pole.

I found a book that promised to address just that: it was called *Five Steps to Overcoming Fear and Self-Doubt*, and it appeared to be just what the doctor ordered. I bought the book, returned to my room to shower off the sweat and dirt from the morning, and then soberly sat down to lunch.

My vacation was turning out to be something very different than I had anticipated. I thought this trip would be a grand celebration of survival and strength after rebuilding from my divorce. I thought the hard part was behind me and that the remainder of my healing would happen easily and naturally. But the devastation I felt when I failed to complete that challenge shook me to the core, and I realized that more work remained. Thankfully, the universe offered me some help.

The book I had chosen was written by Wyatt Webb, one of Miraval's "specialists." Wyatt is a big, tall cowboy kind of guy, and his specialty is people and horses. He helps people better understand how they approach their lives by paying attention to how they interact with a horse.

As I started reading, my inner book critic chimed

in: "Here we go again, another yahoo who thinks he knows everything." I felt stupid for thinking I was going to remedy my fear and self-doubt with a book written by a cowboy, particularly after all I had been through with a guy who thought he was one.

But as I read on, my annoyance had to take a backseat to astonishment when I realized that in this "silly" book, Wyatt frames his discussion of fear and self-doubt around his own experience with a telephone pole on the same challenge course that had brought me face-to-face with myself just a short hour earlier. At the time, I found this coincidence astounding. Since then, I have learned that when I decide to "show up" for my life and pay attention to what is going on around me, "coincidences" like this happen all the time.

At the end of this remarkable book, and after honestly addressing his own fear and self-doubt, Wyatt gives the pole another shot. This time, he gets a very different result. I knew I wanted to do the same—or at least try. On Monday, my last morning at Miraval, another climbing challenge was offered. This one involved a fifty-foot pole with a zip line attached to the top platform. I wasn't optimistic, but I wanted to face my fear while it was still fresh and see if I could effectively manage my fear and self-doubt and finish the challenge.

Monday morning arrived, and I awoke with a feeling of dread. I dragged myself out of bed, threw on some dirty clothes, and trudged out into the beautiful Arizona sun for a morning of fear and self-doubt. I walked through the preliminaries of the challenge largely unconscious. While the facilitators explained the process, my breathing started to become irregular, and my stomach tied itself in knots. We affixed our harnesses, chose our climbing order, and got started. Again, I would be the second climber.

The first climber started out bravely, but just a few feet up the pole, she lost her nerve and climbed back down to the ground. This made me even more nervous.

Now it was my turn. I began slowly, sitting back into the harness a few times to make sure it would hold me. When I reached the ten-foot mark, I started experiencing the same terror and panic I had felt two days earlier. My body shook and my breath quickened. But this time I did not stop. I just "sat" with the fear—allowed myself to be fully present with it. I took deep, slow breaths, and I coached myself up the pole, step by step and breath by breath.

I knew in my heart that if I hung in there with myself, I would be able to do it. I still feel a knot in my stomach when I think about how it felt to be twenty, thirty, forty, and then fifty feet up that pole. It was *terrifying*. But I kept going. I reached the top and stepped onto the platform. I had done it. I was breathless, and I was amazed. My body was trembling, but it had not let me down. I showed up for myself, and that is what got me up that pole.

But, alas, I had only a few moments to celebrate

my grand victory before I realized I had to do just one more little thing, and that was to jump off the fifty-foot platform and ride a zip line back down to the ground. Up until that moment, all I had thought about was getting up that stupid pole. I hadn't even considered that another challenge would face me once I got to the top.

Immediately, all that familiar fear and self-doubt returned. This time, however, it wasn't fear that I wouldn't be strong enough to do it—it was quite simply a fear of letting go. I stood for a long time on the edge of the platform, asking questions, stalling, making excuses, trying to avoid the inevitable. All I had to do was take one little step off the platform, but I resisted it with all my might.

I knew I had to do something. I certainly was *not* going to climb back down, and if I ever wanted to see the inside of Miraval's spa again, I had one choice and one choice only. I had to let go. So I did. And once I took that tiny step off the platform, the rest was easy—and ridiculously fun. I flew through the air awash in sheer joy.

When I returned to solid ground, I was exhilarated. I thought about how close I had come to not trying this challenge and how much fun I would have missed if I had allowed my fear and self-doubt to call the shots. It was a good day.

I left Miraval with a lot to ponder. Although I knew I had taken good care of myself after my separation from Mel, I started to realize that getting back on my feet was just the first step in my healing. I managed to survive and keep a roof over my head, but the work I did at Miraval showed me that I had only just scratched the surface of the pain I was carrying around in me. I didn't have much of an idea about how to tackle this, but I sensed I would have to draw on that same strength I'd managed to find when I got myself up that pole. I showed up for myself on that pole—in both the hanging on and the letting go.

When I got home, I started to pay attention to how fear and self-doubt were impacting my life. I began to notice that when stressful circumstances arose, my instinct was to flee. By removing the stressor, I thought I was removing the pain (good old-fashioned fight-or-flight). Fight hadn't worked in my family or my marriage—mostly because I did not know how to stand up for myself effectively—so flight had become my natural reaction to pain.

Of course, sometimes flight is the healthiest option. I fled my marriage and all that went along with it to keep myself healthy. But now I was out of my marriage and my self-respect and emotional well-being were no longer threatened, so I had to learn how to respond to pain differently. If I wanted to move forward, I would have to find an anchor in myself, learn to sit with pain, and take the time necessary to work through it.

I started to practice just sitting with discomfort. I didn't fight it, and I didn't flee from it. When something in my work or my personal life triggered me, I calmed myself down, took some deep breaths, and identified what was being triggered. Sometimes it was the residual pain of not feeling seen and heard by my family. Sometimes it was the residual pain of being treated disrespectfully in my marriage. Once I started to sort out the triggers, the pain became more manageable and my life started to make more sense. Like those poles at Miraval, the dance of my life is an ongoing process of figuring out when to hang on and when to let go.

Several months after the incident with the poles, I returned to Miraval to do some work with Wyatt Webb, a horse, and fourteen strangers who were on the same journey of self-recovery that I was on. I spent five days in Wyatt's Equine Experience Immersion. It was intense and exhausting, and I would have to write another book to adequately describe how powerful it was for me. There were no handouts, no PowerPoint presentations, and no lectures. It was simply six-hour days in the company of like-minded souls who had the guts to tell the truth about their lives with the help of one very gifted man and one exceptionally patient horse.

It was at the Equine Immersion that I started to address the pain of losing Ted and Ned. I talked about the devastation I feel when I think back on driving down Two Star's driveway for the very last time. When I spoke, people listened. They honored my pain, and they connected with their own losses. And when they told their stories, I connected with their pain, and I realized something magnificent. We are all in this gig of life together so we might as well take the leap and make connections with one another. The experience was transformative. Nine months later, I did the Immersion again because it helped me so much the first time, and I knew I needed it.

There are healing places for everyone. That place might be a church or an Al-Anon group or a yoga class or a cabin on a lake. I have several healing places in my life, but Miraval is unlike any other. There, I immediately relax into myself and find the space and time to focus on my inner work, without distraction, in a supportive environment.

Miraval is not cheap. I know I am incredibly lucky to have the resources to get there once or twice a year, and I work hard to make that happen. Other things take a backseat to Miraval, because, right now, the work I do there is invaluable to me on many, many levels. I am lucky I have Miraval, but I know it doesn't take money to find healing places; it simply takes commitment.

I expect that this process of healing will continue for exactly the rest of my life. At times, I find myself losing patience with the time and effort it takes to live authentically, but when frustrations arise, I remind myself that I no longer want to invest my life in fleeing from and anesthetizing pain. I have more important work to do. I know that the best investment I can make in myself and in the work I do with others is to keep chipping away at the pain that has followed me through much of my life. Wyatt and Miraval help me remember that.

Our Common Pain

When I was a young girl, I sold Girl Scout cookies. Each spring, boxes of Thin Mints, Scot-Teas, and my favorite, the peanut-butter-sandwich cookies then called Savannahs, were delivered to our garage in Edina. There, I sorted the boxes and prepared to deliver them to my many loyal customers.

One day I was sitting on the floor of the garage, studying a box of Thin Mints. On one side of the box was a photograph of several happy, smiling Girl Scouts. Next to the photo were the words, "We have a lot in common." I then turned the box over and found a photograph of a single smiling Girl Scout. Next to this photograph were the words, "There is nobody like me." I flipped the box back and forth, trying to make sense of these two seemingly incongruent messages. I thought, "Okay, girls, which one is it? Either we have a lot in common, or there is nobody like me. Pick a side!"

I have thought back on this internal conversation many times in my adulthood, and over the years I have come to believe that those Girl Scouts had the right idea. We do have a lot in common, but there is nobody like me, and there is nobody like you.

I am certainly no expert on anything other than my own experience, but over the years, I have come to believe that 99.9 percent of the negative and destructive patterns in our lives can be traced back to unhealed pain. This is something we all carry around with us in varying degrees.

People like me, who experienced pain administered by a daily drop of poison, often have difficulty honoring that pain. We are tempted to think that people who have suffered more obvious trauma have a *right* to their pain, and that, in comparison, we have nothing to complain about. This belief pattern can become an endless cycle of denial and paralysis.

I know I have a lot to be thankful for. I have had food on the table every day of my life. I grew up in a nice house in a pleasant neighborhood. I am well educated, I am healthy, and I have wonderful friends and a loving family. There are many, many good things in my life, and I am enormously thankful for every one of them.

But there is also very real and very honest pain, and whenever I feel tempted to sweep that pain under the rug, I remind myself that when I diminish my pain, I also diminish my potential. It takes a lot of energy to suppress this pain, and that energy is much better invested in healing it so I can be fully alive as a friend, daughter, sister, neighbor, and attorney. And I am the only person who can make that happen.

I am helped by tools like therapy and yoga and Miraval, but most of the healing happens when I simply pay attention to my pain when it rears up. I make a place for it at the dinner table, so to speak, and I give it a knife, a fork, a spoon, and a voice. When my pain is triggered, it usually manifests itself in powerful feelings of rage, shame, or fear. When this happens, I take a time-out and try to identify what is being triggered. Once I identify the childhood or adulthood trauma that is being triggered, I find that I almost immediately calm down. When I take the time to understand where these feelings are coming from, it becomes much easier to move beyond them. As the saying goes, "If you can name it, you can tame it."

As I practice naming and honoring my pain, I have noticed that pain no longer hogs the conversation at the dinner table of my life. When I look my pain square in the eye, it doesn't have to jump up and down trying to get my attention, and it no longer has to—consciously or unconsciously—run roughshod over my life. Little by little, it quiets down, and I become more and more free.

This is not easy work. It takes a lot of patience, courage, and tenacity to honestly address pain. It is also not selfish work. In fact, I think it has exactly the opposite effect. The more I chip away at my pain, the kinder, more patient, and less judgmental I become. My pain no longer distracts me from being good to myself and the world around me.

During my first Equine Immersion at Miraval, I started to share my pain with other people. That was a scary and difficult and intimidating experience, but ultimately it became joyous and liberating. When I returned home from Miraval, I continued to tell my story, and when I did, I found that my connections with other people deepened. I also started to feel more and more comfortable in my own skin.

As disjointed and confusing as your own story may seem, when you start sharing it in a safe environment with other like-minded travelers, two things happen. First, the bits and pieces of who you are start to make sense. Once you learn that the pain you carry has a rhyme and a reason, the confusion and dysfunction it creates starts to become more manageable. Second, you learn you are not alone. Your pain does not make you an island. Rather, it makes you a part of humanity.

Your story is yours alone, and that is what makes you one of a kind. Embrace that. Then, open yourself up to the commonality you share with those around you. Share your story, and listen to the stories of others. Embrace both sides of the cookie box, and you will find that safe and exciting place where you can live authentically as yourself while at the same time making honest and healing connections with the world around you. This is what it means to live with your whole heart. It is your birthright and it is available to you every single day of your life. All you have to do is to choose it.

Part Two

What I Learned

While I continue on my own path of healing, I make my living as a divorce attorney. The most valuable things I know about divorce I did not learn from law books. Rather, I learned them from my clients—and from being a client.

Everyone's story is unique, but there are many commonalities in the experience of uncoupling, and over the years, I have discovered some tools that have proven to make the process more manageable for a lot of people—including myself.

Advice is a tricky word, and people facing major transitions such as divorce should be cautious about the advice they solicit and accept. Here, however, I feel I can offer my thoughts and ideas about the challenges of uncoupling in a way that you, the reader, can either accept or reject.

So take what works, leave the rest, and stay on your own path. Nobody knows your situation better than you do. If you trust yourself, take care of yourself, and make good choices, you will find your way.

Trust Your Gut

If something is truly wrong in your relationship, you know this deep in your gut. No matter how hard you may try to ignore it or how persistently you try to talk yourself out of believing they exist, the problems in your relationship will continue to rear their heads until you either completely lose yourself trying to manage them or you reach the point where you decide to address them.

Fear is often the primary reason we don't trust what we know deep inside. When fear consumes your life, there is no room for you to imagine and create a better future. When facing the possibility of divorce, people experience some common fears. These include:

- Fear of disappointing family and friends

- Fear of hurting your children

- Fear of being single

- Fear of an uncertain economic future

- Fear of being wrong

- Fear of change

Anyone who has been in a marriage or intimate partnership knows that a healthy relationship requires a lot of attention and a great deal of give and take. In order for our relationships to work, we have to cut our partners a generous amount of slack—and that has to go both ways. But if the dynamics of a relationship are so out of balance that your safety and self-respect are threatened, it is probably time to wake up and pay attention. Your gut does not have to dictate your choices, but it deserves to be heard.

The bottom line is this: **If you have serious concerns about your relationship and you do not feel safe communicating your concerns to your partner, there is a problem.** You may try to avoid accepting that fact as long as you can, but if your communication is so broken that you cannot be honest with your partner about your deepest needs, you will eventually find yourself with two choices: find the courage to address your concerns in a productive way or consciously elect to spend the rest of your life managing them.

Each choice has its own consequences. If you choose to maintain the status quo, your gut will continue protesting, so you will have to be prepared to invest a lot of energy into coping with that. If you choose to address your concerns, you will likely disrupt your old familiar patterns, and you will have to be prepared to make some major adjustments in your life.

There is no right or wrong choice, and you are the only person who can weigh the costs and benefits of each. Whatever path you choose, however, there is value in living a life consciously chosen rather than an unconscious life dictated by fear.

Give Your Partner an Opportunity to Change

You and your partner have been engaged in the same dance for a long time. You likely have the same arguments, the same impasses, and the same frustrations again and again. If you want your dance to change, you don't have to make a big scene or issue an ultimatum. All you have to do is to stop dancing.

If and when you stop dancing and decide to stand up and tell your partner the truth, you know you are taking a risk because you will have absolutely no control over how your partner will react. But one thing you can count on is this: when you stop dancing, your partner has no choice but to do something different and *something* in your relationship is going to shift.

You may think that if you tell your partner the truth about how you feel, your relationship will automatically end. But that might not be what happens. Sometimes one partner just needs a big wakeup call—like the possibility of a divorce—to get his or her attention. Every now and then, I get a phone call from a client announcing that they and their partner have decided to give reconciliation a shot. I always find this news exciting. It doesn't always stick, but sometimes it does.

When you stop doing the old dance, it is going to feel strange and unfamiliar, and you will probably want nothing more than to get back into that old familiar routine. And your partner will likely, at least initially, beg you to do so. If you do that, however, you will be back where you started, and nothing—absolutely nothing—will change.

And people *can* change. Once one partner changes the dance, the other partner has to decide if he or she will dance alone or whether he or she will try a new dance too. If both partners find the courage to do this, a relationship has a chance to heal.

In my situation, Mel was not about to change any part of how he conducted himself in our marriage, and when I stopped dancing, he pretty much sprinted off to find a more compliant dance partner. I was left on the dance floor all alone, and I was terrified. I could very easily have chased after him, apologized for "overreacting," and then invested another ten or twenty or thirty years in walking on eggshells.

Fortunately, I had enough seeds of strength in my heart to remain honest with myself, and I did not chase after him. It was the most difficult choice I had ever made, but when I made it—and stuck with it—the old and familiar and agonizing dance was finally over, and I was free. I just had to get to the point where I was willing to risk losing the familiar, well-established dysfunction.

As you contemplate this risk, it is important to remember that this is not just about you; it is about *both* of you. Chances are, if you are unhappy in your relationship, your partner is also unhappy. Sometimes the most loving thing one partner can do for the other is to tell the real, honest, difficult truth. This enables both of you to live happier and more authentic lives, whether that means learning how to dance together or apart.

Accept Responsibility

A wise man once told me, "You are 100 percent responsible for 50 percent of every relationship you are in—no more and no less."

This is not about the division of labor in a relationship, and it is not about assigning blame. Rather, it is about understanding how much power you have to effectuate change and taking responsibility for the half you can influence, while giving your partner space to take care of their half.

There were times in my own marriage when I took on too much responsibility for our troubles. I thought that if I changed enough about myself, our marriage would get better. There were also times when I wanted to blame Mel for all our problems, and I was tempted to relinquish responsibility for my share. But when I started to take care of my half—no more and no less—Mel had space to show me what he could or could not contribute to our relationship. And that gave me a great deal of clarity about our marriage and the person I had married. It also gave me a lot of clarity about what I was contributing to our problems.

Most people bring their best selves and all their good intentions to their marriages. Even so, we have to come to terms with the fact that we each also bring our share of vulnerabilities and shortcomings. Acknowledging what we contribute to the difficulties in our partnerships is the humbling and honest first step in building well-functioning adult relationships.

It is sobering for me to admit how much emotional immaturity I brought into my marriage. I was an educated woman in my early forties, and I was living my life as an adult in just about every respect. I might have looked like an adult on the outside, but inside lived a terrified child who just wanted to be loved-and that sweet, terrified child pretty much called the shots when it came to how I participated in my marriage.

When I was growing up, I thought I would be loved if I worked hard enough to make sure everyone around me was happy. I continued that pattern into my adulthood and into my marriage. I allowed my needs and desires to take a backseat to Mel's needs and desires, and that created an imbalance that could not be sustained without taking an enormous toll on my own self-esteem and on the health of our relationship. Self-awareness changed everything.

When you learn to take full responsibility for 50

percent of each relationship you are in—no more and no less—you create space for your partner to take responsibility for their share. **If both partners are willing to do this, balance can be restored, and relationships can thrive.** If your partner is unable or unwilling to take care of his or her part, you can decide whether you are willing to live with the imbalance this creates or whether it is a better choice to let go and move on. If you choose to let go, you can move forward knowing you did the best you could with the part of the relationship you had the power to influence.

Gather Support

If you end up on the road to separation or divorce, you will not be able to manage the transition—whatever form it takes—on your own. You need support. Accept that. Be cautious, however, where you solicit that support.

Choose your early support carefully. Oftentimes, close family members and friends are not your best choice as your most intimate confidantes and advisors. Those closest to you have a lot invested in your marriage, and their emotions will inevitably interfere with any support and advice they offer you—whether you are pursuing reconciliation or divorce.

A better choice, especially in the early days, is a good, solid therapist. If you can't find the courage to do anything else, find a therapist who will support you, challenge you, and give you the confidential assistance you need while you sort out your options for the future.

If money is an issue, look around your community. Most communities have resources available for free or reduced-fee counseling. Most health insurance policies provide coverage for counseling. Explore your options. Therapy is a tremendous tool.

If therapy is not an option, look at Al-Anon or Adult Children groups. Particularly with Adult Children, you do not need to have a family history that involves alcoholism to participate in these groups. Attendees simply have a history of living in a dysfunctional family, regardless of whether that dysfunction was caused by alcohol abuse. These groups require only a small suggested donation, and the support you receive will likely prove invaluable.

In addition to getting a therapist or support group on board, it is vitally important that you surround yourself with people and activities that nurture you. Consciously decide that you are going to take care of yourself. Create something of a cocoon. Feed yourself well, exercise, and get enough sleep. Whatever contributes to your well-being, *do it*. You have to be your own best friend. If you don't yet feel you deserve to do it for yourself, do it for your children or for that small child within you who deserves to be cared for.

When your world feels upside down, it is easy to forget to take care of yourself. Be gentle with yourself, but at the same time, take the time you need every day to keep yourself healthy and supported—inside and out. This may be the most important commitment you make during a very challenging period of your life. Don't let yourself down.

Assemble Your Professional Team

When the time comes to find an attorney to help you, choose carefully. Every client has different needs, and it is essential that you find an attorney suited to meet yours. Some people do not need a lot of handholding, but many do. If you know you need emotional support, choose an attorney who has the time and the capacity to give you this. When you interview attorneys, be as clear as you can about what you need and carefully consider whether you think they can offer this to you.

Again, your gut is your best guide. Don't hire the first attorney you meet just because you want to cross that difficult task off your list. It takes time and fortitude to find the right person to guide you through this transition, and I encourage you to make that investment. Many attorneys offer a free or reduced-fee consultation for prospective clients. Take advantage of this. You will learn a lot about the process, and you will learn a lot about yourself.

Today, people have many options when they are considering divorce. These include collaborative divorce, cooperative divorce, mediation, traditional litigation, or a combination of the above. Having all these options can be confusing, but it is worthwhile to explore them. When you are interviewing attorneys, ask them about the modalities they use. Educate yourself about the options. Find the attorney and the modality that best fit your situation.

I am comfortable practicing all of the modalities mentioned above. Some attorneys are not. Many attorneys choose to limit their practice to one or two modalities, and this is often a legitimate professional preference. Problems arise, however, when attorneys think their way is the only way and they are intent on selling their point of view to everyone who walks through their doorway. Any attorney who believes he or she has all the answers clearly does not. Every case is different, and every case requires a customized approach.

When clients are interviewing me, I am also interviewing them. I want it to be a good fit for both of us. If our goals and styles are not compatible, the relationship will not work. Some attorneys are so focused on bringing in new clients that they will take on everyone who comes along, and they will tell potential clients what they think they want to hear. Trust your intuition and sift through the bravado.

Strange as it may sound, I believe family law attorneys are in the business of helping families heal. Many attorneys don't see it this way, and they think they are serving the best interests of their clients by fueling conflict. Some divorce attorneys are aggressive. They serve papers, file motions, posture, and approach every little thing with an unnecessarily adversarial attitude. Think long-term when you choose professionals to guide you through the process.

If your attorney is encouraging you to write a vicious affidavit, for example, you need to know there may be long term consequences from doing so. Many attorneys are not going to tell you that your divorce records are available to anyone who has the time and inclination to read them, so if you choose to air your dirty laundry in court records, you may very well have a large audience for your troubles. Once the initial pain from whatever wrongs you have suffered has faded into the distance, your court records remain, and they are just sitting there waiting for your friends, neighbors, colleagues, employers, and *your children* to read them.

At a time when your emotions are running high and your attorney suggests an aggressive move, it can be very difficult to resist going along with the program. But beware of the attorney who is more interested in stirring the pot than truly helping you.

Helping you means this:

1. I hear you.

2. I want the best for you.

3. I am going to help you get there by coaching you to make good choices along the way.

Having a law degree does not guarantee emotional intelligence, and I am often surprised by how lacking in emotional intelligence many attorneys are. It doesn't take a rocket scientist to know that when a party or an attorney comes out of the gate in an aggressive, over-reaching manner, the opposing party will become reactive and defensive, and this serves only to drive the parties further apart. By the time a couple reaches the point of divorce, there is usually a fair amount of acrimony between them, and the last thing they need is for the legal process to escalate this. Although divorce is never easy, a well-managed divorce should *diminish* acrimony, not intensify it.

In my early days of practice, pretty much every divorce was litigated—often fiercely. It was just how things were done. Attorneys were very oppositional. We did not communicate well with each other, and we tended to be more focused on *winning* than on truly helping.

Over time, however, I started to see that whether clients thought they "won" or "lost," those who fought their way through the process usually found themselves more damaged at the end than they were at the beginning. Fighting is a very different thing from strength, and fighting without clear intention will take an enormous toll on you and everyone around you.

Fortunately, the climate of aggression has started to soften in recent years. Part of this change was prompted by courts being incredibly overburdened. This created a tremendous need for alternative dispute resolution processes. The other contributing factor, I believe, was that clients were getting smarter. People began to see the fallout from bitterly contested divorces, and they started to demand alternatives.

Although the formal collaborative divorce process doesn't work for everyone, it is a good option for many people. In a collaborative divorce, the parties and their attorneys sign an agreement stating they will work toward reaching full settlement without court intervention. They also agree that they will be completely transparent with each other. All information is exchanged voluntarily, and neutral specialists assist with parenting and financial issues. If settlement is not reached collaboratively, both attorneys must withdraw from the case, and the parties have to hire new attorneys and start the case over. A cooperative divorce is similar, but without the attorney disqualification provision.

There is some backlash in the legal establishment against movements such as collaborative and cooperative divorce that seek to lessen the adversarial nature of the process and encourage clients to explore the deeper aspects of uncoupling. Dissenters claim that these approaches undermine their obligation to zealously represent their clients and that the confines of these processes pressure people to accept unfair settlements. I disagree. Clients are adults, and as long as they fully understand the process they have chosen, they have every right to proceed in the manner that works best for them and their families.

In my own divorce, I knew there was no possible way these modalities would have worked. First, Mel does not operate from a place of collaboration. He wants to conquer and win. Second, these processes require a high level of trust between partners—something we did not have. I knew my marriage better than anyone else and I knew what would work and what wouldn't work.

What did work for us was utilizing a neutral financial expert. One of the most useful and valuable trends in family law practice in recent years is the use of neutral experts—in collaborative and cooperative cases as well as litigated cases.

There are neutral experts who work with financial matters and neutral experts who work with parenting issues. **Financial neutrals can very efficiently do the legwork to sort out your financial picture with respect to property valuation and division, cash flow, and maximizing the tax effects of both.** When children are involved, neutral child specialists can provide essential assistance to parents as they craft parenting plans. Child specialists come in many forms, and their titles are different in every state. These experts help parents focus on the best interests of their children. **Neutral** child specialists coach clients to view their parenting obligations as privileges, not rights, and they work with them to create parenting arrangements that work best for their family.

Many people who are in a great deal of pain allow their and their children's long-term happiness to take a backseat to their anger. This is where the negative effects of divorce happen. Although there are very few absolutes in the divorce process, this is one: Don't ask your children to manage discord between their parents, because they are completely unequipped to do this. Any adult who grew up witnessing their parents criticize and disparage each other will tell you how damaging and confusing these messages can be.

Your attorney can steer you toward the neutral professionals he or she recommends for your particular case. These professionals can save you a great deal of money and needless conflict, even in the most acrimonious divorces.

It takes a lot of courage and a lot of self-control to accomplish what I call "the good divorce." **The healthiest divorces happen when both parties effectively manage their emotions and approach the process with the intention to do the best they can for themselves and their families.** The right professional team can help you accomplish this.

You have a choice when it comes to inviting professionals to join your team, and I encourage you to choose professionals who see you as a multifaceted person, not just an income source or an opportunity to demonstrate how tough and crafty they are. **This is a time for you to strive to be your best self. Assemble a professional team that can help you be that.**

Tame Your Greek Chorus

During all our major life transitions, people seem to come out of the woodwork to offer us advice. Whether we are getting married, having a baby, getting a divorce, or caring for aging parents, everyone has something they want to say about it. We all have our own "Greek chorus"—the family members, friends, and colleagues who want to advise us and help us. Although almost universally well-meaning, a large percentage of this advice and these stories fall into the category of "Not Helpful."

As soon as you tell others about your uncoupling, you have to be very clear about what you need from them and how they can support you. Although it is not always easy to limit the size of the audience that witnesses your transition, you can decide whether you will make room in your brain and your heart for every story and every piece of advice you hear. If you take in everything that comes along, you will soon find yourself overwhelmed, confused, and lost. You have to set limits.

For the most part, the advice you need from family and friends should focus solely on your emotional well-being—it should not be legal advice. If you have a reliable professional team behind you, there is no need to get legal advice from anyone else.

Every day, people come to my office with scary stories their friends and family members have told them about divorce. Most of these tales came from good-hearted people who care. In the retelling, however, many facts have been distorted, and most often, these stories have little or nothing to do with reality. A good attorney can help you separate fact from fiction so you will know what actually warrants your concern and what doesn't.

If you find yourself questioning the advice of your team, get a second opinion from another qualified family law attorney Maybe get a third opinion. It's one thing to recognize when a shake-up is needed in your legal team, but allowing amateurs to influence such a choice is quite another.

If your Greek chorus insists on inserting itself into your process, you are the only person who can set limits. The words "Thank you, but that is not helpful" have rescued many people from the black hole of fear and self-doubt that opens up when you make room for every piece of advice that is offered to you.

Friends and family members who truly care about

you will appreciate your honesty. They *want* to help you; they just don't always know how to do it. It is up to you to coach them in the most helpful direction. This is one time in your life when you absolutely do *not* need to take in everything offered to you. So keep your Greek chorus in its proper place—at the back of the stage.

Manage Worry

If I had a nickel for every email and phone call I received from Heather during the twelve-month odyssey that was her divorce, I wouldn't be *wealthy*, but I'd have a pretty good stash of latte money to last me the next twenty to thirty years.

Heather had challenges. After an eighteen-year marriage, her husband abruptly left her because he decided in his mid-forties that he wanted to have children—but not with Heather. Heather was devastated, and while struggling with this unexpected loss, she also had to figure out how she was going to piece together a future.

Heather had health problems that prevented her from working during much of her marriage, so when her marriage ended, she was absolutely paralyzed by the prospect of a financial future without her husband.

Early on, Heather's worries were out of control. It was not unusual for me to turn on my computer in the morning and find ten to fifteen emails from her. When my phone rang, there was about a 75 percent chance it was from Heather. During the night, Heather expressed her worry in long, heartfelt emails to me. By morning, however, she would often feel differently, and she'd beg me to disregard everything she had written. Then, the next night she was back into her worry.

Heather's Greek chorus was big, and she was continually inviting new members to the stage. One day after we had settled all the major issues in the divorce, Heather spoke to a stranger at a coffee shop who told her she was *crazy* not to insist upon taking an interest in her husband's business. I knew the business was not a reliable asset for Heather and that her involvement in it would keep her tied to her husband indefinitely, which would prove to be enormously difficult for her. Accordingly, we had put other, more stable assets in her column, along with generous lifetime spousal support. Heather had understood this, and she had agreed with all settlement decisions. But after talking to that one stranger, she wanted to take everything off the table and start over.

I managed to coach Heather into accepting the settlement I believed was best for her, but she was so prone to worry that she continued to have doubts before, during, and even after the final settlement.

It's natural to worry as you go through the process of uncoupling, but if worry is allowed to go unchecked, it will consume your life. **When working with** worry-prone clients, I often advise them to schedule a two-hour block once or twice a week as dedicated "worry time." Then, when they wake in the middle of the night, distraught about how their kids are going to adjust or whether they can pay their bills or how they will move forward once they are single, they can remind themselves that they have scheduled time to worry on, say, Tuesday morning from 8:00 to 10:00. That means they can let it go for the time being and get some sleep. It sounds silly, but it works.

When I was working with Heather, she was completely stalled with worry about how her future would look. She could not imagine living anywhere without her husband. At one of our meetings, I became so frustrated with her that I told her to put on her coat and get in my car. We went apartment hunting. I wanted to show her there were options out there. Of course, I can't do this for every client, but I had the time and inclination to give her a little extra help because it was early on in my new practice, and Heather was the sister of a dear friend of mine.

Ultimately, Heather ended up in a beautiful old apartment in a historic area of Saint Paul. The space she created there was absolutely fantastic—and so different from the suburban life she shared with her husband. All she needed was a little nudge to set the worry aside and see for herself what her future could be.

If you are worry-prone and you want to get through

this process with any semblance of sanity, you *have* to learn to manage worry. There is no magic way to eliminate worry, but the process for learning to manage it is simple. **You manage worry by letting go of it every single time it rears its head. Just as you would not allow an intruder in your home, you cannot allow worry to take root in your mind.**

This takes practice, and until it becomes more natural for you, you will likely have many opportunities to practice letting go of worry every day. If you remain committed to this practice, it will get easier. It helps to remind yourself that worry accomplishes nothing helpful. It actually moves you in the wrong direction. Unmanaged worry will suck the strength right out of you, and this is time when you need as much strength as you can muster. So practice, practice, practice. Invest your energy into self-care, not self-destruction.

Take Charge of
Your Finances

One of the most common worries during the process of uncoupling is money. Many people remain in abusive or otherwise unhealthy relationships because they are worried about money. Much of this worry is based on nothing more than vague fear that can be managed by doing a little bit of legwork.

However challenging your financial circumstances may appear to be, don't assume money alone has to keep you from living the life you want to live. Take the reins of your finances, educate yourself, and decide that you are not going to let worry derail you. Then, when you have done your homework, the decision about whether to stay in your relationship will be an educated one— and not a default decision based upon what may prove to be unfounded fear.

In most marriages, one partner has more

involvement with financial matters than the other. This is usually a very normal and practical division of labor, and just because one partner hasn't historically managed the day-to-day finances doesn't mean he or she cannot learn how to do so. It is not a mountain to climb; it is simply a very manageable learning curve. Basic money management is not terribly difficult, and learning how to do it will bolster your strength and your self-esteem. You might just need some help, and there is *plenty* of help out there.

Your first task should be to put together a monthly budget. This may sound like an overwhelming and depressing exercise. But in my experience, once clients overcome that initial resistance, they find this exercise empowering. Many even find it fun. Budgeting gives you the opportunity to envision what your future might look like, and it forces you to consider what is really important and what might not be so important.

The first budget I suggest you put together should be based on your historic spending over the past year. There are many budget worksheets available on the Internet and through your attorney or financial planner. These worksheets can be very helpful, but they can also be overwhelming. If you feel overwhelmed, ask for help. Your attorney and your financial advisor are experts on budgets, and they have lots of helpful tools to offer you. **Asking for help may feel foreign to you, but if you want to become proficient in taking care of yourself,**

you have to learn to ask for help when you need it.

When I was doing my budget, I didn't use a worksheet. I found that it was easier to make up my own format based on my credit card and checking account records. I went through every single charge and every single check or cash withdrawal over a period of one year. I did the entire thing in an afternoon with a Twins game on the radio, and believe it or not, I enjoyed it.

Mel and I shared a credit card and a checking account, but it was remarkably easy to figure out which charges were mine and which were his. Mel tended to shop at his stores, and I tended to shop at mine. When I looked through my statements, I realized I spent money in the same places every month: Target, the grocery store, and the drugstore, for example. So when I did my budget, rather than having individual lines for household supplies, groceries, and toiletries, I simply included lines for Target, the grocery store, and the drug-store. I added up my annual expenditures at each store, deducted about 25 percent to account for the fact that I would be supporting a household of one rather than two, and I divided by twelve to determine my monthly spending. For expenses paid in cash, I didn't labor over how much I spent on coffee or parking or the occasional fast-food lunch. I simply added up all the cash withdrawals from my checking account over the year and then divided by twelve. It took me about twenty minutes to determine that I went through roughly $200 in cash each month.

When it comes to your children's expenses, I suggest that you put these in a separate column. Aside from your mortgage or rent, groceries, and utilities (which are more accurately treated as overhead), allocation of additional expenses for your children will be determined in the course of your divorce. So, to the extent possible, keep your children's expenses, such as lessons, clothing, camps, childcare, and sports equipment, separate from your own.

Of course, budgeting is not an exact science. You might not be able to get a firm handle on your budget just from your spending history. Some things will require some speculation. When Mel and I separated, I had absolutely no idea where I would end up living. I knew I wanted to purchase a house and that I wanted to stay in Saint Paul, so I prepared a budget that reflected household expenses commensurate with living in a house of approximately the size (modest) and age (old) of our Saint Paul home. I looked at real estate listings and estimated a purchase price and a down payment, and I based utility expenses on our current home. This proved to be close enough.

You will probably find it much easier than you imagine to estimate what it will cost you to live as you move forward. Just by managing your life all these years, you have built up a wealth of knowledge about what it takes to financially support yourself and your children. Your budget doesn't have to be exact. For the time being, it just has to be in the ballpark.

Once you have finished this first budget, you will probably have the confidence to branch out a bit. Visualize different scenarios for your future. Early on in the process, you, like me, may have little certainty about how your future may look. If this is the case, put together several budgets representing different scenarios, especially when it comes to your living arrangements. One budget might reflect staying in your current house. A second might be based upon purchasing a different home. A third could reflect the cost of renting a home. Visualizing and budgeting different scenarios is not only important; it can also be exciting.

Once you get your budgets together, it is time to look at your income. Try to figure out what, if anything, you will need to bridge the gap between your various budget scenarios and your own income. Financial planners, tax preparers, and attorneys have computer programs that can help you calculate your net monthly income based on a variety of tax scenarios. Take advantage of these resources. They can save you a lot of time and frustration.

If you will need additional income to meet your anticipated budget, talk with your attorney about child support and spousal support. Get the information you need to determine what, if anything, you may need from your spouse. This should be one of the very first conversations you have with your attorney. Your well-chosen attorney will guide you through the additional financial issues that need to be addressed in the divorce.

If you do some of the financial legwork before your partner knows you are contemplating divorce, be careful about whom you consult regarding your financial matters. For example, if you share an insurance agent (which most couples do), ask another agent to give you coverage estimates. Always ask for confidentiality. You do not want your partner to find out from anyone other than you that you are doing some investigation.

Money can be scary to those of us who haven't spent a lot of time managing it, but like everything else important in life, it is a worthwhile investment of your time and energy to understand the basics. You do not have to master the stock market or the inner workings of the Federal Reserve; all you have to do is figure how much money has to come in to support what goes out and how much you have to save each month to prepare for the future. This is not rocket science; it is a basic skill that you can master. The best advice I can offer is to keep it simple, take one step at a time, and ask for help-because there is a ton of help out there. Ask for help from your attorney, your financial planner, your friends and family, community education, and the Internet. You can do this.

Accept Realignment

One thing I don't think I fully understood at the time of my separation from Mel was that it wasn't just an ending for Mel and me; it was also an ending for everyone who was invested in our marriage. While I was scrambling to manage my own pain, friends and family members had to figure out how they too were going to move forward after our divorce.

Of course, my own close friends and family members were stalwart allies throughout, never wavering in their support. But as time went by, I started to notice that some of our couple friends were becoming distant, and I had to come to terms with the fact that many people I held dear had chosen Mel over me.

In the beginning, I had been naïve enough to believe that people could stay friends with both of us, and that they didn't have to abandon one of us in order to stay friends with the other. Over time, however, I learned to accept the fact that realignment was inevitable. Everyone had to make the choices that worked best for them, and these choices were not necessarily a negative reflection on me. It was widely known that Mel could hold a grudge, and I expect that when a choice had to be made, it was just easier and safer for many of these people to let me go.

While some friendships faded to the background, there were some unexpected surprises. Pat, Elizabeth, and Joan—initially "couple friends"—made it clear to me from day one that they were not going anywhere. They rallied around me as soon as they learned about our separation, and they absolutely refused to let me fold up into myself. They invited me to church events and dinner parties and plays. They took me along on weekend getaways. They gave me room to vent and occasions to laugh. At the same time, they did not let me drown in self-pity.

Betsy was another surprise. Betsy was an old friend of Mel's, and when everything blew up, she decided that history alone was not going to dictate whom she chose as her friend. Betsy is a highly regarded business consultant in the Twin Cities, and when she learned I was starting my own law practice, she volunteered to coach me. Many times I would arrive home from work to find an inspiring article in my mailbox from Betsy, along with a note encouraging me to find my voice and blaze my own trail.

And then there was Carolyn. Carolyn had met Mel

several years earlier while they were serving together on a charity board, and this was where I later met her too. I didn't know her well at all, but I had spent time with her at events, we volunteered at the same children's shelter, and we seemed to like each other a lot. When Carolyn learned of our separation, she called me every week to check in and see how I was doing. It may have been a small gesture, but it was a powerful one for me because I felt seen and heard by someone who mattered. Carolyn reminded me that despite Mel's larger-than-life persona, I was not invisible.

If you allow realignment to take place without judgment, you will understand how powerful it is when people decide to support you at a time when they could very easily do otherwise. Support often comes from the least expected places—embrace it. At a time when you may be struggling to show up for yourself, it is an indescribable gift when someone else makes the decision to be there for you.

In her beautiful poem "Kindness," Naomi Shihab Nye writes, "Before you know what kindness really is you must lose things." I read that poem many years ago, but it was only after I suffered big losses of my own that I started to understand what her words meant.

As difficult as loss can be, it can also be a great teacher. But if you stay fixated on your pain and allow resentment to build because of the choices other people make, you blind yourself to the positive things loss can teach you. Once you get to the other side of a major struggle such as a divorce, you will understand pain and loss better, and that can be an unexpected gift.

Arthritis taught me a great deal about what it is like to live with chronic pain. Now, rather than feeling annoyed by people who move through life at a slower pace than I do, I find myself much more inclined to offer these people kindness and empathy. I understand that they might be moving slowly because they are in tremendous pain. I never would have understood this if it weren't for my own experience with chronic pain.

My divorce taught me how powerful gestures of kindness and support, both big and small, could be during a very difficult time in my life. Every voice of support that came to me in the wilderness of my loss was a balm that supported my survival and my healing, and I will never forget how powerful that was. These lessons learned from loss empower me to offer more kindness and forgiveness to others—and also to myself. And that has been an indescribable gift.

Accept realignment as best you can, embrace the support that is offered to you, and open yourself to the idea that loss has something valuable to teach you. This probably won't happen right away. But as you move forward with your life, and as you have the time and space to process the changes on a deeper level, you can take these lessons of loss down from the shelf and learn from them.

Claim Your Territory
(and Choose Your Battles)

You and your partner not only share relationships, you also share places, experiences, and possessions. Everything that has been important in your relationship is also subject to realignment. When the time comes to decide what you want to keep and what you are willing to let go, make heart-driven choices.

During our marriage, Mel and I attended a large annual charitable event in the Twin Cities. We had many friends who shared our commitment to this charity, and we knew dozens of people who attended every year.

A short time after Mel and I separated, this event rolled around. I was so busy adjusting to my new life that I didn't even remember it was happening. But Elizabeth, Joan, and Pat did remember, and they purchased a table for ten that included a spot for me. They decided I was going to attend, whether I wanted to or not. They would not let me surrender this event to Mel without an effort.

When the night of the gala arrived, I was nervous. I hadn't been to an event involving so many of our friends since our separation, and I knew Mel would be there. From the moment we arrived, my posse was on high alert. Husbands and dates were enlisted as my protectors, and they refused to leave me alone for even a minute. They watched vigilantly to make sure there were no accidental encounters with Mel. I didn't think I needed all this protection, but then I saw Mel strutting around the room in his cowboy hat with his "latest" on his arm. My stomach turned inside out, and I was grateful to have so much support around me.

The sight of Mel making such a display of himself so soon after our separation was repellent to me, but my feelings had nothing to do with jealousy. I had *no* desire to be the woman on Mel's arm. What I felt was embarrassment. I was embarrassed for myself. I was embarrassed for Mel. And I was embarrassed for that poor woman on Mel's arm, with her big hair and shiny prom dress. But mostly, I was embarrassed for our friends who had to witness this spectacle.

I lasted about an hour; that was all I could take. I said my good-byes to my understanding friends, caught a cab, and went home. Henry and Prickly Pete greeted me at the door. I spent the rest of the evening on the couch, watching old movies with a bowl of popcorn on my lap. I was happy and at peace, and it was such a relief to be out of that circus. I made a good effort, but I learned that the event was not something I needed to claim. Mel got this one, and that was fine with me.

Mel also got our church. When our priest learned I would no longer be attending, he encouraged me to stand up for myself and not allow Mel to take it from me. Similarly, friends fervently encouraged me to fight for the ranch and the horses and all the *stuff* we had. They cared about me, and they did not want Mel to flatten me with his steamroller.

I appreciated their support, but when it came to choosing what I would fight for, I trusted my own heart. Rather than listening to my Greek chorus, however well intentioned, I listened to myself, and I made the choices that were right for me.

Many things, such as our church and our charities, were relatively easy to let go. South Dakota was much more difficult. Just a few short weeks after we separated and Mel returned home from the hospital, he and I met at our Saint Paul house so I could remove the remainder of my belongings. While sorting through my mail, I came across a strategically placed photograph of Mel in a warm embrace with a woman with long brown hair and a whole lot of makeup. I felt a pang.

Mel watched me from across the room. Without looking up, I said, "Please do me one little favor. Until the divorce is final, please don't bring any women to Two Star." Mel was silent. I looked up at him. He had a sly smile on his face, and that said it all. My request was already too late, and even if I had made it earlier, he still would not have honored it.

Although Mel had not even fully recovered from his accident, he was already busily dating. This didn't surprise me. What did surprise me was how quickly I had to accept the fact that these other women were sleeping in our bed at Two Star under the beautiful red quilt I helped design. Strangers were being invited into *my* sacred space.

Up until then, I had assumed my clothes were still hanging in the closet and my boots were still lined up in the front hall. I thought Two Star would remain neutral territory—at least for the short term. I now realized that my belongings had probably been stuffed into garbage bags and thrown into the basement to clear the way for Mel's new life. I later learned my assumption was correct, when those garbage bags were unceremoniously delivered to my front porch in the middle of the night.

To this day, my heart aches when I think about losing Two Star, Ted, and our South Dakota life. Not a day goes by when I don't miss those five hundred acres of prairie and all that went along with them. I expect this loss will remain with me until the day I die. But I know it was just something I had to let go of so I could be free.

There was one place I was not willing to give up, however, and that was the Lexington. "The Lex," as it is known, is an old Saint Paul restaurant with a rich and storied history. The Lex is a noisy, clubby place with reliable food and great martinis. It was close to our house, and during our marriage, Mel and I dined there frequently. We knew the managers and the staff, and we always felt at home there. Every night at the Lex was special. I loved that place—and I was not going to let Mel take it from me.

After our separation, I staked my claim at the Lex. I made a point to dine there at least once a week. Sometimes I took friends, but most often I went alone with a book. I loved those dinners, and I felt completely comfortable. I ran into Mel from time to time, usually with a flashy date, but it didn't rattle me. I found my book and my martini much more interesting than anything Mel was up to, and it felt good to stand (or, rather, sit) my ground.

One evening, several months after our divorce was final, I was dining with a friend at the Lex, when Mel walked in with a very, very blonde woman flaunting an engagement ring. The staff dutifully came to their table and did the appropriate fawning. Then they walked by my table and rolled their eyes, silently reassuring me of their true sentiments.

And believe it or not, I was not bothered by this much at all. I actually found it kind of amusing. All I remember thinking was that I was *so* glad I wasn't that woman. And although she didn't much look like the ranch type, I hoped with all my heart that she would love and take care of our Two Star. I had every reason to believe she was a good person who was probably as in love with the "greenhouse" as I had been, and I was relieved Mel had found someone else to take care of him. It was not a great night, but it was not a terrible night either. Getting through it with a smile, rather than tears, showed me how far I had come.

Despite Mel's best efforts to claim the Lex as his own, I did not give it up. I continue to go there as often as I can. I still run into Mel and his latest from time to time, but that is never more than a minor annoyance. Mel is not going to take the Lex from me. Of course, it's just a restaurant, but it means something more to me. Claiming the Lex means I can make my own choices and I can claim what I want to keep while letting other things go.

Fighting battles and staking claims just for the sake of winning is a waste of time and energy. Make heart-driven choices. **Stake your claim in the places and things you want because you truly want them—not because you want to punish your partner or prove how "strong" you are.** Invest in the things you truly care about and will be able to maintain into the future. If you cling to every little thing you have lost, you will never be free. I lost Two Star, but I got my freedom and the Lex, and that turned out to be enough.

Make Good Choices

When I start working with new clients, I often tell them my goal is to get them to the end of the process in the best possible shape emotionally and financially. In order to get them there, we have to—in South Dakota terms—keep the "white hat" on their heads. This is often difficult for clients to understand, because it means they have to make thoughtful, reasoned choices at a time when they are usually more inclined to simply react to their pain.

There is a lot of research out there about how people make decisions during times of great stress. **In sum, you can't count on yourself to make solid decisions when your brain is flooded with emotion.** So work with your support team to process and manage your emotions and when it comes to making good strategic decisions, allow yourself to be coached.

When one partner insists on being aggressive and oppositional, it can be enormously difficult for the other partner to resist acting in kind. In most instances, however, choosing to be reactive serves only to move everything in a destructive direction. It also slows down the process and escalates the acrimony.

I often tell my clients, "I have a bulldog in my backyard, and I'm not afraid to bring her out if I have to." Rarely, however, is this necessary. When difficulties arise, I find I can usually accomplish much more by simply being clear than by barking out threats.

Fighting for what you believe is right might feel empowering for a short time, but it is probably not worth a gigantic legal bill and a mountain of residual resentment that will affect you long into the future.

One of my goals in my own divorce was to leave the marriage from a position of strength rather than victimization. This goal was not about fighting, taking rigid positions, or venting in front of mediators and judges. It was also not about getting "more." My intention was simply to not allow fear, intimidation, and exhaustion to prompt me to accept less than what was fair. It was a balancing act, and I had to check in with myself regularly to make sure my decisions were consistent with my goals. My attorney did not provide much in the way of coaching, but I learned how to coach myself.

Early on in the process, clients often have questions about what they need to do to "protect" themselves financially. Inevitably, their Greek choruses have advised them to transfer some assets or do something else so their partners don't "clean them out."

When people ask me about such things, I ask whether they are genuinely concerned that their partners will cut them off financially or dissipate their assets. Most often, the answer to this question is no. If this is the case, they don't have to clean out a bank account to protect themselves. In reality, aggressive financial moves tend to create a dynamic of mistrust and trigger reactive behavior. Soon, everything spirals in a negative direction that is nearly impossible to reverse. Furthermore, if one partner does make an inappropriate transfer of assets during the process, he or she will be held accountable for that as the divorce progresses.

This is not to say that you should blindly trust someone who has already proven him-or herself untrustworthy. The time came during my own divorce, before I was earning enough money to support myself, when Mel's erratic behavior and threats to withhold money from me caused me some very real concern. Of course, the money Mel earned went to him alone, and no withdrawals could be made from our joint accounts without mutual consent. I relied on Mel to help me pay my monthly expenses. I had a hefty mortgage payment, and I was investing a lot of money into starting my law practice. I was concerned.

When my concerns reached the point where I felt action was needed, after much consideration, I withdrew some money from our joint line of credit (the only joint account both of us could still access) and deposited it into my own bank account. Mel was livid when he found this out, but in retrospect, it was one of the best choices I could have made. It completely shifted the balance of power. Mel was no longer able to hold me hostage by threatening to withhold money from me. This was the best decision for me, but it was a risky move. Be careful when you consider choices like this.

When you make decisions about your children, be especially cautious, because your actions affect not only you and your partner, but also your children. I am continually inspired by strong and courageous clients who decide that, despite whatever poor choices their spouses may make, *they* are going to keep the white hat firmly on their heads and do the right thing for their children.

The wife of one of my clients decided it was a good choice to videotape my client every time he came to her house to pick up their young daughters. Apparently, she thought she was building some sort of "record" against him by documenting the occasional rough transition—a common experience with young children during parental exchanges.

It wasn't easy for my client to tolerate this humiliation every time he came to get his kids, but he sucked it up again and again. And when all was said and done, he ended up in a much better place financially—and, more importantly, with his daughters—than his wife did. He had the courage to make good choices. He refused to engage in the drama his wife was creating, and his self-control paid off.

His ex-wife, on the other hand, ended up with an enormous legal bill and, I expect, a future filled with pain and unresolved anger. She made a poor choice, and it had consequences. At the end of the process, it was clear to the judge who decided the case that this woman cared more about her version of justice than about the well-being of her children. In all my years of practice, I have never seen a person more invested in her personal pain than this woman. She was so completely blinded by her pain that she lost all sight of the best interests of her children.

The challenges you face as a result of the divorce process itself are relatively short-lived, and these challenges do not define who you are now or who you will be in the future. If you invest all your energy into your pain, the damage you inflict on yourself and your children will take much longer to heal, and it will prolong the time it will take for you to move forward. You and your children deserve better.

If your case is litigated, and you have a history of making good choices while your spouse goes in another direction, the judge who hears your case will inevitably see the truth. Judges are not naïve. They deal with divorces almost every day, and they have seen it all. I don't think there is anything judges disdain more than litigants who play games, insult their partners, and use the divorce process to air dirty laundry.

When the care and custody of children are at stake, judges are looking for the parent who is best able to facilitate a positive, healthy relationship between the children and *both* parents. Parents who come to court with hateful accusations against their partners are, in most cases, hurting only themselves. If a judge is forced to make a decision about which parent should be the primary custodian for children, she or he will be much more likely to choose the parent who has demonstrated good judgment and the strength of character to stay out of the cesspool of anger and hate.

When times get tough, strive to keep the white hat firmly on your head. This can be challenging, but in the long run, your good choices will pay off.

Recognize Your Blind Spots

When I was in law school, United States Supreme Court Justice Anthony Kennedy spoke to my class. During the question-and-answer period, a classmate asked Justice Kennedy how he wanted to be remembered as a justice. He considered the question for a few moments and then responded, "I want to be remembered as a person who was not afraid to see his own blind spots."

This answer impressed me. I was inspired to know that someone in a position of such great power did not live his life believing he had all the answers. Rather, Justice Kennedy viewed his life as a journey of continual learning. He kept his mind and heart open to new ideas and different ways of thinking. There and then, I promised myself I would strive to live my life the same way.

Clients often come to me with very rigid ideas about what is right, what is wrong, and how everything should play out in their divorces. Most of these convictions come from a place of anger, hurt, and despair—and they are often fueled by a robust Greek chorus. Clients who find themselves stuck in rigidity need to be reminded that feelings change, time heals, and in order to move forward, they might have to soften their convictions, look at the bigger picture, and open themselves to a larger reality. They also have to get to the place where they are willing to look at their own blind spots. Although your emotions deserve to be respected during the divorce process, they also have to be managed.

I give my clients a fairly wide berth when it comes to venting, but sometimes the venting gets to the point where it interferes with my ability to help them. Not only is it a poor use of my time to invest hour after hour helping clients process and manage their emotions (that job is much better handled by a therapist), but it also detracts from my ability to be an effective advocate, because their pain and rage build anxiety in me. When my own feelings of fight-or-flight are triggered, my decision making becomes clouded.

Several years ago, I had a challenging client named Manny. Manny was largely estranged from his two teenage daughters. I don't know all the dynamics that played into that estrangement, but I did know that Manny was looking to everyone but himself to heal his relationship with his daughters.

Manny lived in Seattle. His wife and daughters

lived in Minnesota. Manny called his daughters infrequently. He came to Minnesota to see them only once over a period of eight months.

When Manny first contacted me, he instructed me to do what had to be done to get his daughters to Seattle for the month of August. It was already mid-June, and the chances of accomplishing this without his wife's cooperation were slim to none. Nevertheless, Manny believed that just because he decided he wanted to be a father again, the court would intervene and get him what he needed.

I suggested to Manny that he start by coming to Minnesota to see the girls—maybe take them on a short trip and start rebuilding their relationship. This was not what he wanted to hear. He demanded that I take "quick and decisive action to get my girls to Seattle in August, like I instructed." Manny fancied himself to be a powerful person and as his agitation escalated, he told me he was prepared to solicit the help of the United States Supreme Court and "the highest offices of government" to ensure that "justice would prevail" and his daughters would be shipped to Seattle in August.

I did not know what to do with Manny. There was no possible way I could meet his expectations, and I had little hope I could get him back on track. I was on the cusp of withdrawing from the case, but before doing so, I had a heart-to-heart with Manny.

I told Manny flat out that even if a Supreme Court

hearing was an option (which it wasn't), nine strangers (or perhaps I referred to them as "eggheads") in Washington were not going to heal his relationship with his daughters. I couldn't fix it, the courts couldn't fix it, and the "highest offices of government" couldn't fix it. The only person who could heal his relationship with his daughters was *him*.

I know this was extremely difficult for Manny to hear, and I fully expected he would hang up on me. But much to my surprise, he listened. Manny loved his daughters, but he was angry with their mother. He felt totally screwed by the entire situation, and his instinct was to lash out and assign blame. Manny believed that if he could prove to the world that he was *right*, his relationship with his daughters would magically be fixed.

Manny turned out to be coachable. He was willing to recognize his own blind spots. It took time, but Manny started to let go of his anger. He started focusing on what his daughters needed, rather than on what his unhealed pain and anger were dictating. Over time, Manny found the courage to do what needed to be done to rebuild his relationship with his daughters. This took tremendous patience and a great deal of humility on his part, but he got there. A court didn't do it, the legal process didn't do it, and I didn't do it. Manny did it. And when he started to address his own pain, he got back what was most important to him: his daughters.

Look at the Big Picture

During periods of change and upheaval, it can be hard to remember to step out of the craziness swirling around us and take a look at the bigger picture of our lives.

A few weeks before I finished writing this book, I found myself at the end of a difficult morning, feeling inextricably frustrated and paralyzed. I was stuck in my writing, I was stuck in my practice, and I felt stuck in pretty much every aspect of my life. I didn't seem able to generate any kind of forward movement with anything.

Cases weren't getting settled, the book was refusing to finish itself, and my house and my office were a mess. As I spent the morning battling this exasperating inertia, I started to question everything about what I was doing and how I was managing my life. At lunchtime, I had the good sense to give myself a physical break from the phone and the email and the negativity, and I gave myself some time to regroup.

I grabbed a legal pad and a pen, and I walked to

the neighborhood café down the street from my office, which is aptly named The Neighborhood Cafe. I sat down at my little table, ordered my lunch, and looked down at that blank legal pad. I sat there for a few minutes and then asked myself this question: "What would help me right now?" Soon the idea came to me to draw a picture of my life.

I drew a large square on the middle of the page, and I looked at it for several moments. The words of my friend Mike Elsass, a gifted painter and Miraval's artist-in-residence, came to mind, and I reminded myself to put "brush before brain"—or, in my case, "pen before brain." I decided not to think about what I was going to draw. I just started to draw.

In the center of the large square, I drew a small circle, and inside it I wrote "Me." I then drew a wavy line across the middle of the page from left to right, but not cutting through the small circle on the middle of the page. The wavy line resembled an ocean supporting the small buoy that was "Me."

Above the wavy line, I drew several small pictures. I drew my house, the pretty French doors in the entryway to my office, and my trusty car. I also drew numerous small faces and figures representing neighbors, colleagues, friends, and family members.

Then, in small circles placed between these pictures, I wrote the words "Yoga," "Law Practice," "Therapy," "Publishing," "Bank Accounts," "Bills," "Charitable Work," and "Obligations"—all the things I tend to every day.

Then I looked below the line and wrote these phrases: "My deepest drives," "My unique purpose on this planet," "The big picture of my life," "The mystery I cannot understand or control," and "My soul's journey that must unfold in its own way and time."

Around these phrases I drew more small circles, and in them I wrote, "Dreams," "Writing," "Miraval," "Telling the Truth," and "Lanterns" (meaning those special people who have found their way into my life and offer me guidance—people like Wyatt and Mike Elsass and the many other teachers who help me along the journey).

Finally, outside the big square that contained these drawings and words, I drew small animal figures at each corner and along the four sides of the square. These represented Ted and Ned, the therapy horses I worked with at Miraval, and Henry and Prickly Pete. These are my animal protectors—my "familiars," as they are known in ancient cultures—the beings and spirits that surround me and protect me.

I put down my pen, and my lunch arrived. While I ate, I took some time to observe what I had drawn. As I took it all in, an enormous feeling of relief washed over me. Seeing my life represented in this primitive drawing prompted a dramatic shift not only in my day but in my overall outlook on my life.

In recent days, I had been defining myself by my

"above-the-line" life—the things above the ocean horizon in the drawing. This included the perceived success or failure of my practice, the fact that Henry and Prickly Pete were overdue for their vet visits, and my inability to finish this book.

I realized I had been trying to dislodge my inertia by evaluating, judging, and juggling my above-the-line life, without regard to the fact that something might be shifting in my life represented below the line. This paralysis did not necessarily mean something above the line needed to be "fixed." It just meant that I might have to ride the wave of the shift, manage as best I could those things I could influence, and give the below-the-line changes time to resettle. This was an enormous relief.

I know that my above-the-line life is important and it deserves to be carefully tended, because there lie the things that hold me in the world and support the mystery that is unfolding below the line. My work, my friends, my family, my neighbors, and my house give my life context, while the deeper spiritual part of my existence evolves below the line.

Although I might see glimpses of this below-the-line mystery from time to time, I know it is not within my human capacity to fully understand it. As the apostle Paul writes in the first book of Corinthians, this is that part of my life that I can only see dimly—as if looking through a murky, foggy window. **Honoring this below-the-line, foggy image of who I am—without fully**

understanding it—is, for me, the definition of faith.

As I finished that lunch, I turned the page on my legal pad and wrote down my own version of the Serenity Prayer: "God, help me make good choices with the things I can influence, help me let go of the things I cannot understand or control, and remind me to create space for both of them to exist without judgment."

This calming shift in perspective helps me more fully embrace what is going on in my above-the-line life while still holding space for the mystery that is unfolding below. When I remind myself that I cannot control all the ups and downs in my life, I am much more able to appreciate the things in my above-the-line world, and I am relieved of the inevitable disappointment that would arise if I allowed those things to define the quality of my life.

Feeling unbalanced or "stuck" from time to time does not necessarily mean you are doing anything wrong. This is particularly true when you are trying to manage all the disruptions that take place during the process of uncoupling. You cannot manage everything in your life perfectly. **Not only are shifts continually taking place in your above-the-line-life, but there are also shifts taking place below the surface, and many times all you can do is to support those shifts as best you can without judgment.**

Pursue Happiness

At my first yoga class, our instructor offered this little nugget of wisdom: "Everything you need to be happy and free is already inside you." I snickered a bit and thought, *Whatever, kid. It can't possibly be that easy.*

Well, it is not easy, but I now believe it is true. After my separation from Mel, the unexpected happiness that flooded through me while I sat on the floor in that empty condo did not come from anywhere outside of myself. After all, I had just lost everything on the outside that I thought was important: my marriage, Two Star, our horses, and my life as I knew it. I had little more in my possession than a knife, a fork, and a spoon.

Rather, the happiness I felt at that difficult time came from somewhere deep inside me. It was simply a very real sense of joy in just being me—something I had not felt for a very long time. This was worth infinitely more to me than any material thing I might have lost. I knew I would love Ted and Ned and Two Star for the rest of my life, but

I also knew I did not have to *own* them to love them.

While that sense of deep happiness remains, so does the pain. I continue to struggle with the loss of Two Star, and it is nearly impossible for me to imagine entering another intimate relationship. But I resist judgment about the things that challenge me, and I simply make room for my pain to exist and heal. I also take my own advice every day. I keep putting one foot in front of the other in the direction that feels truest, and I allow the chips to fall where they may. Like my experience on those poles at Miraval, my life is a process of continually figuring out when to hang on and when to let go.

As I practice mindfulness in my work, my yoga practice, my friendships, and my daily life, one of the wonderful surprises is that I find I am much easier on myself. I cut myself more slack. I am no longer plagued by the self-judgment that followed me throughout much of my life. I laugh at myself much more, and I sleep much better at night.

I also notice I am more comfortable in the world. Although I am constantly reminded of those bits and pieces of myself that I am not crazy about, overall, I really like myself quite a lot. I am good company. I crack myself up. I am fun, I am reasonably smart, and I care about the people around me. Although in some ways I am still my worst critic, I now feel as if I am also my biggest fan.

Life continues to be as challenging and frustrating

and happy and sad as it has always been, but at the same time, everything is different. Now I know there is a big, strong, steady river that runs through it—and that is my big and difficult and flawed and wonderful authentic self, who can now live and breathe and take up space in both my above-the-line life and my below-the-line life.

I continue to disappoint myself fairly regularly, and I wake up every day knowing I will make mistakes. But I am much more inclined to laugh at that and let it go. I know when I get up in the morning that, whatever happens, I can count on myself to allow the journey that is my life to take me where it needs to go.

I know I won't make it up every pole that lands in my path, but I also know that when challenges arise, I can count on myself to at least show up. And whether or not I make it up any given pole, I know someone will be waiting on the ground to give me a pat on the back, laugh at my mistakes, give me a big hug, and get on with lunch and the spa. And that person is *me*.

As I write this, it is midnight, and I am sitting on my bed in my warm little house in Saint Paul while a beautiful snowfall swirls outside. I feel as if I am in a tree house in a snow globe. Henry and Prickly Pete, my dear protectors, are sleeping beside me. And as I watch the snow, I am reminded of Ted, with whom I shared many lovely hours walking through the prairie on nights like this. I hope with all my heart that he is warm and content somewhere in South Dakota, and I have to trust he is.

I sit here in the middle of this beautiful snowfall, and I think about what I have seen so far and all I have yet to discover. These words come to mind, as Robert Frost's words often do:

The woods are lovely, dark and deep.
But I have promises to keep,
And miles to go before I sleep,
And miles to go before I sleep.

I do have miles to go before I sleep, and I have many promises to keep, both for myself and for the people I care about. I know there are many challenges ahead, but the road is so much easier now because I have found so much strength inside of me. Through all the twists and turns to come, I know I can rely on myself to be fully present for my life. And that is, quite honestly, the greatest gift I have ever been given.

Turns out my yoga instructor was right: I do have everything I need to be happy and free already inside of me. And so do you.

Notes

Notes